Praise for

NO ASHES IN THE FIRE

"Darnell Moore is one of the most influential black writers and thinkers of our time—a beautiful, intentionally complex feminist activist writing liberatory futures. I cannot wait for the world to read *No Ashes in the Fire*."

—Janet Mock, author of *Redefining Realness* and *Surpassing Certainty*

"*No Ashes in the Fire* is part memoir, part social commentary. Darnell honestly tells his story with an intensity and passion that offers readers a deep understanding of a gay black male coming of age who open-heartedly claims his identity, and who embraces redemptive suffering. Ultimately, he reaches out to everyone with an inclusive love." —bell hooks

"Darnell Moore is doing something we've never seen in American literature. He's not just texturing a life, a place, and a movement while all three are in flux; Darnell is memorializing and reckoning with a life, place, and movement that are targeted by the worst parts of our nation. He never loses sight of the importance of love, honesty, and organization on his journey. We need this book more than, or as much as we've needed any book this century."

—Kiese Laymon, author of *How to Slowly Kill Yourself and Others in America*

"Radical black love is the major force for black freedom, as so powerfully embodied and enacted in Darnell Moore's courageous book. From Camden, New Jersey, as a youth, to Brooklyn, New York, as an adult, Moore takes us on his torturous yet triumphant journey through racist and homophobic America. Don't miss his inspiring story!" —Dr. Cornel West

"*No Ashes in the Fire* is everything that is quintessentially Darnell Moore: brilliant, courageous, transparent, and wholly original. Moore's masterful writing feels like equal parts soul music and gospel testimony. With this book, Moore positions himself as one of the leading public intellectuals of our generation. More importantly, he has written a text that will inspire, and maybe even save, many lives."
—Marc Lamont Hill, author of *Nobody: Casualties of America's War on the Vulnerable, from Ferguson to Flint and Beyond*

"Darnell Moore's *No Ashes in the Fire* is a searing, tender, and wise memoir. It is the captivating story of a man, a family, a community, and an age in the life of Black America in which old wounds and new possibilities meet at an earth-shaking crossroads. Moore is a reflective, contemplative, and instructive scribe. His are the words of an organizer, a social historian, and a fighter with a deep love for his people."
—Imani Perry, Hughes-Rogers Professor of African American Studies, Princeton University

"In *No Ashes in the Fire*, Darnell Moore takes a single life—his own—to prove the principle of intersectionality: the so-called issues we'd like to push away from ourselves, those supposed other worlds we claim to only encounter on the news, are indeed the actual individual lives we lead. Moore shows us how he, and therefore each and every one of us, grapples with the myths surrounding sexuality, race, class, and loneliness. Or as Moore himself writes, 'I lost myself because I had longed so badly to be found.' No one goes unscathed, but on the other hand, no one goes untouched. This is a book of experience and survival."

—Jericho Brown, author of *The New Testament*

NO
ASHES
IN THE
FIRE

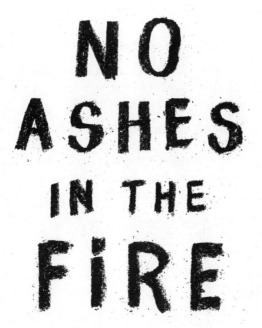

NO ASHES IN THE FIRE

Coming of Age
Black & Free in America

DARNELL L. MOORE

NATION
BOOKS
New York

Nation Books
116 East 16th Street, 8th Floor
New York, NY 10003
www.nationbooks.org
@NationBooks

Printed in the United States of America

First Edition: May 2018

Published by Nation Books, an imprint of Perseus Books, LLC, a subsidiary of Hachette Book Group, Inc. Nation Books is a copublishing venture of the Nation Institute and Perseus Books.

The Hachette Speakers Bureau provides a wide range of authors for speaking events. To find out more, go to www.hachettespeakersbureau.com or call (866) 376-6591.

The publisher is not responsible for websites (or their content) that are not owned by the publisher.

Photos accompanying the Prologue and Chapters 1 through 8 courtesy of the author. Photo accompanying the Epilogue courtesy of Regina Langley.

Print book interior design by Jouve

Library of Congress Cataloging-in-Publication Data has been applied for.

ISBNs: 978-1-56858-948-0 (hardcover), 978-1-56858-949-7 (ebook)

LSC-H

10   9   8   7   6   5   4   3   2   1

Our humanity is illuminated by our brokenness as much as it is by our capacity to put ourselves back together over and over again. To the men whose lives were shaped by the beautiful complexity that made them human: I have written this book in memory of you. George Lewis and Grafton Harrity, thank you for giving me life. I will remember you always.

CONTENTS

PROLOGUE

S miles were not rare during my childhood. They were not hidden. But I would never have remembered the joy, emanating through my big grin, had I not returned to my mama's worn photos of me a few years ago.

Some of the pictures were baked by sunlight. I scattered them across my bed and looked at faded images of a thin black boy whose glasses rested on a head too big for his body, hiding eyes that were windows into a world more fantastic than the world he moved through. Long crew socks with colorful stripes covered scrawny legs that were gifts, and not only because they allowed him to run from bullies. He played hide-and-go-seek and rode Big Wheels over dirt mounds just as often as he would fold his body into itself when it was time to hide away.

I once knew this black boy in the photos, but at some point between growing up and breaking down I had forgotten. I could not recall his imaginative spark and infectious laugh or the sound of his desperate prayers for perfect grades tossed into the universe as if he was aware of his powers.

Thirty years later, I looked at the photos with keen interest in my bedroom in Bed-Stuy in Brooklyn, miles away from Camden, New Jersey, the city that was the backdrop of this black boy's life. I was in awe. To laugh and jeer during days punctuated by fear was a feat. What childlike magic did he use to make it through? And how did I get so far away from him, so distant from that smile? I had forgotten my days were not always rocked by violence. It did not occur to me that play would be more evident than struggle. The signposts of happier days were etched on my face in my mama's pictures.

I started to remember how I would tap into the strength I didn't know I had to turn the days following sleepless nights, pierced by my dad's loud punches and my mom's screams, into new opportunities to forget and move forward. My hours of play outside with my cousins and friends provided opportunities to dream about the worlds we could explore beyond cement parks or dirt front yards. Somehow we learned to appreciate all we had and did not realize all we lacked.

But how did I forget?

Memory is a tricky force, especially when brutality, poverty, self-hatred, and many other unseen hands, which turn beautiful people into monsters and victims, dictate what we remember. I blocked out memories so I could sleep at night. Many I forgot so I would not kill myself or the monsters in my life. I forgot, too, in order to avoid facing the monster I was becoming. And in my room, on my bed, close to my mama's pictures, and closer to that little black boy than I've been in a long time, I felt compelled to find him once again, to recover what I had lost, especially the joy.

This book is a search for self. While looking over my mama's pictures, I wanted to remember the parts of my journey

I had forgotten. Every word and every sentence that follows is an attempt to recover the parts of myself I stared at in the photos, the many smiles and moments of joy hiding behind the walls trauma left. It is also a quest for history, because we come to be the people we are within the context of a larger world ruled by powerful, insidious forces. The long, collective hatred of blackness, the calculated policing of sexual difference, the intentional ghettoization of urban centers, and the lure of the American dollar are just a few of the strong forces that shaped my senses of self and the way I viewed others. Each chapter is a scene, a snapshot of my life, and an attempt at traversing time in search of the lessons I now know were present. Writing this book has allowed me to look back and recover memories I thought I had lost and recall moments I tried my best to strangle. I return to places I've been many times before. Each return is a dance with memory.

IT TOOK YEARS BEFORE I realized the image in my mama's pictures was beautiful. With skin too brown, big lips, and a wide nose, I often turned away from my reflection. As I grew up, there were invisible forces moving about like ghosted hands. A hand would touch my cheek and steer my head and eyes away from the mirror. It was unseen, but felt. It needed to be named.

I never knew I was poor, lived in a ghetto, or was looked upon as a number waiting to be keyed into a statistical formula when playing school on my grandparents' porch in Camden.

Riding public transportation from the pothole-lined streets of Camden to my Quaker high school two hours away in the posh suburbs didn't terrify me. But the one time I rode home in my white ninth-grade English teacher's car, along with my white middle-class suburban classmates, was dreadful. A hand covered my eyes so I could not sense my confounded class-mates' astonishment, my cowering presence, and the tight grip of shame that needed to be named.

What strong fist pounded away at my desires and beauti-ful thoughts of a stranger, a boy, holding me so close that I would feel, faintly, his own breath? What force stopped my heart from fluttering, my body from perspiring, my internal light from burning? The force was unseen, but felt. I didn't understand then why it had its grip on me, but I know now that it needed to be named.

To discover and name what shapes us is to engage in the work of history. I knew writing an honest memoir would require me to tell the truth about my life, which has been full of hostility and splendor. Discovering the difference between what's true and all the lies one comes to believe requires a direct confrontation with the past. Long before I was born and Camden was made out to be a city full of dilapidated homes, violent drug dealers, crack, and nihilism, bureaucrats and greedy businesspeople en-acted racist public policies and brokered shady deals, transform-ing our home into a city tapped of its resources and hope.

Stereotyping black urban cities like Camden as "ghetto" and the people who live within them as leeches sucking the state dry of its capital are lies forged without a commitment to history. If Camden is a ghetto, it is because some force, comprised of many hands, made it so. That, too, must be named.

I am a black man who has loved and been intimate with men and women, a black man who defies societal norms, a black man who grew up in the age of hip-hop and AIDS, and a black man from the hood. I couldn't write a memoir full of life stories without animating all the invisible, and not-so-hidden, forces that rendered my blackness criminal, my black manhood vile, my black queerness sinful, and my black city hood. This book is testimony; it is a cultural and political history bringing to light the life of a black boy maneuvering through a city whose past he never knew. But it also an emotional history, a search for the many ghosts that haunted my heart and spirit, and whose stealth presences were as palpable as damaging policies and trigger-happy police officers.

My thoughts, however, are not the definitive take on blackness, manhood, and sexual politics. How can it be when my path, choices, struggles, triumphs, failures, questions, and answers are my own? My words are my attempt at joining a chorus of voices who have tried their best to narrate the beautiful and messy complexities of race, gender, class, and sexuality as they collide and are expressed in the contemporary United States. This work, then, both is and isn't about me. It's a book I wanted to read because too many books have yet to be written by and about the rich experiences of black people who are forced to survive on the edges of the margins because they choose to love differently, refuse standards of so-called respectability, make less money, talk more shit, or deny the state its power.

Memoir can provide an entryway into the life of the writer. On the journey, readers might run up against some semblance of their own lives captured in the sentences of another's story. This memoir is an invitation into my world as best as I can remember it existing. My black life, however, is lived as a consequence of the lives of so many others. I hope to honor their lives and narratives, too. In all the years of my white and heterosexual-oriented K-12 schooling, and during my five years as a struggling undergraduate student at a Catholic university, I went without reading books reflecting any part of the black life I had experienced. Black lesbian girls, transgender brothers, gay fathers, and bisexual lovers were not central characters invoked in mainstream fiction, nor were their lives examined in any discussion I had in my classes. I didn't learn about the works of Audre Lorde, Barbara Smith, Essex Hemphill, Marlon Riggs, Marsha P. Johnson, and Cheryl Clarke until I searched for them in my late twenties.

As I wrote this book, I remembered the vast congregation of the black dead who have been taken from us. I remembered fifteen-year-old Sakia Gunn, a lesbian from Newark, New Jersey, who was stabbed to death by a twenty-nine-year-old man whose advances she rejected. And seventeen-year-old Wauynee Wallace, who was shot in the back of his head while walking through the neighborhood in Camden I grew up in. And

Eyricka Morgan, a black transgender woman from Newark slain at the age of twenty-three, a few years after she and I became friends, a few years after she participated in Newark's first intergenerational queer oral history conference, and a short time before she would have graduated from Rutgers University. And Gregory Beauchamp, Tiffany Berry, Desean Bowman, Terrance "Jawan" Wright, Islan Nettles, Adolphus Simmons, and Simmie Lewis "Beyoncé" Williams Jr. All the dead lived lives before they were killed. They created friendships, fell in love, made others the butt of their jokes, and dreamt. They breathed, thrived, and made an impression upon us.

I've been haunted by these deaths since I learned of them. They constantly make me question whose stories are allowed to flourish in our collective memory and whose are blotted out. This book is a response to the call emanating from their graves. It's a demand for collective freedom and life. And it is a way of saying: we are here.

Those black LGBTQ people were killed because they were courageous enough to reveal the unseen hands that ball up in the form of a fist when confronted with difference. Sometimes the hand is black. Their display of out-loud self-love, their bold naming of their queer and transgender identities, and the force of their fists swinging as they attempted to dodge the blows or bullets from their attackers have become sound waves and a perpetual reminder that they lived. And live still. Their stories are not mine to exploit nor are their stories those of martyrs whose deaths were a necessary lesson. I retell them here because it is important to understand how particular aspects of black urban life teach us that it takes unmatched agility to survive under conditions that make so many of our unnatural deaths possible. This is especially true of those of us growing up black, queer, and transgender in places like Camden. And because of this reality, so many of us forget we once smiled big before others attempted to snatch our smile away. My words are a reminder of our existence and our joys.

This story is not new. And my story is not unique. Black queer, transgender, and gender nonconforming people in America are bearers of narratives of struggle and triumph despite the ways intimates and strangers have attempted to force us to silence our sexual desires. Our stories, like our lives, are complex, bountiful, profound, disappointing, hopeful, varied, and often disregarded.

We have always been here. Black queer, transgender, and gender nonconforming people loved and fucked on some racist master's plantation. We wrote theories debunking white racial supremacist ideology. We, too, were architects of Black liberation, women's justice, antiwar movements, and the Black arts. We are the unnamed black sisters, brothers, and non-binary people who lived queer theory before it was popular among those in white academe.

We are James Baldwin, Jackie "Moms" Mabley, Richard Bruce Nugent, Bayard Rustin, Pauli Murray, June Jordan, and so many more. But in 2018, these are the names some still refuse to remember and celebrate.

Prologue

We are the alive. The dead. Lovers. Fighters. Movement builders. Cultural producers. We are the everyday, ordinary magicians who learn to create life amid death-dealing cultures of hatred and lies. We maroon ourselves. And we birth freedom, but many of us are still denied our rightful place in the master narratives of Black history and American life. Even in these progressive, Afro-futuristic-oriented times, our life stories and contributions are still refused. And that is why we must tell as many of our stories as we can. *No Ashes in the Fire* is mine.

Chapter 1

PASSAGE

The first home I recall living in as a child was at 1863 Broadway. The year was 1980. I bounced around the modest two-story brick row house in South Camden like a typical four-year-old not yet blessed with the company of a horde of cousins who would eventually come after me, taking the place of the imaginary friends I conjured in my mind. My maternal grandparents, Jean and George, had purchased the house in the late 1970s using their meager income.

My grandmother, whose beige skin was dotted by dark brown freckles, tripled as the primary caretaker of the children, student at Camden County College, and instructor at the nearby Mt. Olive Day Care Center, where I was also a pupil. She graduated with an associate's degree in elementary education. My grandfather, whose dancing brown eyes drew you in to his cocoa-colored face, was a custodian at the Beta House in Camden and at Bancroft Inc. in the suburb of Haddonfield, New Jersey. Both were organizations serving people with developmental disabilities. But outside of the hard manual labor he did over the course of long days, he was also a poet. His love of words, however, was veiled. I didn't know that we shared this passion until, many years later, I stumbled upon his elegiac verses in a scrapbook. I only remembered the graceful way he moved around our house, much like an artist scanning the world for inspiration.

We didn't have much in that house aside from an over-abundance of furniture. Too many faux porcelain plates in the honeycomb-brown armoire with glass doors and ersatz silver handles. Too many slightly chipped knickknacks and magazines and pieces of mail sitting alongside the usually empty faux-crystal punch bowl on the matching buffet table. Too much wallpaper peeling, showcasing paint and, like a palimpsest, yesteryear's scribble on tattered walls. Too many people, which meant there was too much love and there were too many arguments, which made our house a hospitable and electrifying communal space for family and friends despite its humble conditions.

Our family of eleven made do in the three-bedroom house. The few concrete steps and tiny, cement backyard were our havens for play and gatherings. My grandparents slept in one room, "the girls" were split between the two remaining rooms upstairs, and "the boys" slept in the basement. The names of my mother, aunts, and uncles—Diane, Ruth, Arlene, Ella Mae, Barbara Jean, Lorraine, Stephen, and Mark—were often yelled throughout the day, followed by a command to clean up, cease bickering, or walk to the neighborhood store. I was the eleventh member to be added. My nickname, Nelly, would be called out just as often.

Our house was located near the city's shipyard and walking distance from the county's trash incinerator plant and

Camden city's waste management facilities. The stench of overcooked trash in Camden, our roughly ten-square-mile hometown of an estimated 87,000 people, was normal. South Camden smelled like a steamy concoction of about half a million residents' shit and weeks-old rotten food shipped from the suburbs to the county trash incinerator in my neighborhood. If Camden smelled, it wasn't the fault of city residents. The trash incinerator was built in Camden because it was a predominantly black and Latino city. It not only polluted the air with a nauseous smell but also contributed to asthma and other illnesses. It's simply what we had to endure.

Camden neighborhoods, like those of many Northern cities, were once highly segregated. Italians were the dominant community living in our neighborhood. The Whitman Park neighborhood was home to a mostly Polish community. Jewish residents lived in the Parkside and East Camden sections. North Camden was home to Irish, German, and Italian residents. And German residents lived in the Cramer Hill neighborhood. By the time I was born, the city was mostly black, but remnants of its past segregation were palpable. In the 1980s, Camden residents still used clichéd nicknames when referencing neighborhoods. The Fairview neighborhood in South Camden was called "White Boy Fairview," and Whitman Park on the west side of the city was known as "Polack Town." When I was growing up, Camden was stereotyped as a black and Latino ghetto infected by an ostensibly pathological strain of blackness. But that's not how I understood

17

blackness as a child. In my home and on my block, the sounds of giggling black youth and the smells of late-summer barbecues in my black neighbors' backyards lessened the impact of the ruckus and the putrid smell that might have impeded the black joy we channeled.

The dance battles my mom and aunts held in our living room, for example, were as lively as any on *Soul Train*. As music blazed from boom boxes, the six black girls would shake and lift their skinny legs, cloaked by wide-legged jeans, with deliberate rhythm. I would watch and imitate their moves with precision. As they slid across the floor with twisted smiles and sweaty foreheads, the teens probably forgot about the woes that came from collectively raising the family's first baby or the times my Aunt Arlene would lead a few of her siblings to the supermarket and steal enough food to fill a shopping cart. To this day, whenever I hear the percussive opening of Sugar Hill Gang's 1981 party-starting hip-hop anthem, "Apache (Jump On It)," I still remember the happiness and the spirit of unbreakable kinship present when they danced together hard enough to strain a bone. My family members had a home and each other, if nothing else. But beyond our home in South Camden, I did not know my family had put down and then lost roots in other parts of the city as well.

THE THIN LINES ETCHED across her forehead and circling her eyes, which were as russet and deep as the rivers of the South Jersey Pinelands, were evidence of the lessons that had made her stronger and wiser over the course of her many years. I didn't know much else, including her full name, as a child. But I knew that my great-grandma, Elpernia Lewis, preferred the company of her children and grandkids, and sodas.

As a kid, I traveled alongside my mom and aunts, skipping a few steps ahead, as they talked in the kind of secretive manner teens feigning adulthood tend to perfect. We would stop into a corner store, stocked with minimal goods, where they purchased 16-ounce glass bottles of Sunkist orange sodas to give to Elpernia. Shopping at corner stores had to suffice because there wasn't a supermarket within walking distance.

When we finally entered her government-subsidized townhouse, complete with white furniture and lightly painted walls the color of eggshells, we would encounter modesty. Her house was clean and bare, smelling of simple living and the hair grease my mom and aunts would use as they pressed her long silver hair. Outside her house were brick-laid housing projects, liquor stores, and black churches. In the 1980s she lived in a housing complex named Allen Nimmo Court because the home she once owned was lost to foreclosure.

As a child, I always found her silence indecipherable. But I suspect now that her forlorn disposition as an elder had much to do with the atrophy of all she and her family had worked so hard to accumulate over her many years. My family mastered the art of locking away secrets. I searched digital archives to learn my great-grandmother's maiden name, the names of her parents, her date and place of birth, and the date she lost her home. I searched because I wanted to understand my family's history—my history. Stumbling through the present unaware of the people and circumstances from which I came was like walking in the dark. I know my life began at a particular point in time, in a particular place, but I was not aware of the path my elders had traveled to get me there. As I researched, I studied the signatures of three generations of family members on military registration cards and marriage certificates. Every curve and fracture spotted in their handwriting resembled an inkblot, giving hints about the disposition of the people who existed in the world I had often imagined but never traveled through. The contexts in which they survived were complex and inspiring. The racism, economic exploitation, misogyny, and political disenfranchisement that tried to suffocate their hopes and block their passage to realized freedom were present, but the forces did not always succeed. And even when they did, our family's unmatched love seemed to always triumph.

Elpernia was born in 1907 in Spotsylvania County in northern Virginia. In the early 1920s, she traveled to Philadelphia with her mother Julia Johnson Lewis, who had been born in 1887. Back in Spotsylvania, Julia was a cook who had not attended school but still learned to read and write. Her husband, John Henry Lewis, born in 1877, was a carpenter and farmer. John's death in 1917 is still shrouded in mystery, but it is the reason Julia and her daughter Elpernia left Virginia and the superficially serene southern way of life they were used to—a world where careful speech and rigid rules of courtesy only amplified the lurid racism, racial segregation, and Jim Crow laws restricting black freedom and well-being.

Some of my great-aunts believe John was killed in a coalmining accident in Virginia, but his death certificate lists pneumonia and influenza as causes. Either explanation is plausible, given the influenza pandemic that tore through the nation in 1918. And it was equally possible that white business owners who did not value John's life and labor could have covered up the accidental death of a low-wage working black man in Virginia in 1917. John's premature death is one example of how fragile black bodies can become when overworked and undervalued. Forty is too young to be buried. As a forty-year-old, third-generation grandson of a black man who died without seeing his children grow up or his dreams fully realized, I know this to be true. Knowing he had died so young, having left so much behind, at the same age I was when I first learned his name and stared in awe at his signature on legal documents, shook me. His early death was a reminder of the unpredictability of black survival in the United States. I spent many days believing I would never live past twenty-five, let alone forty. But I did. I wonder if he thought the same.

Digging into my maternal family's history provoked questions. I wanted to know how Julia and Elpernia experienced their movement from the miles upon miles of green pasture in Virginia to the blocks upon blocks of narrow brick row houses they would encounter in Philadelphia. While researching, I discovered the mother and daughter initially found lodging at Miss Berty's Boarding House, but I wanted to know more about Miss Berty. Was she black? Was she a fair landlord? Did she pound on their door at the start of each week or month demanding rent? Julia remarried in 1922 and had three more children, but I imagined Elpernia's face, that of a black woman whose eyes blazed with confidence, focused on her new father figure with a glare of youthful suspicion. I imagined Elpernia moving about the home the growing family moved to after they left the boarding house, looking like her granddaughter, my mother, with glossy cocoa skin, hair dark and shiny as onyx, and a face lit by a calculated smile. When I met her in her early seventies, she moved about as if she were a mystery—never physically commanding and talkative, but always fully present and spiritually prevailing. Her quiet presence intrigued me; there was so much I wanted to know about her. I had questions. Why, for example, did someone code her race as "mulatto" on the 1910 census when she was a three-year-old living in Virginia, but code her race as "negro" on the census of 1940 when she was thirty-three, married, and mother to four kids, including my maternal grandfather, George, in Pennsylvania?

During the 1940s, Elpernia was employed as a domestic worker. According to her 1940 census records, she worked sixty hours a week. Twenty hours more than I am required to work at my job today, Elpernia labored to feed her children and create opportunities they may not have had otherwise. During World War II, she worked at the Philadelphia Quartermasters

Depot, where clothing and flags were made for the US military. She, like her mother before her, worked long hours in domestic and other low-wage, high-performance positions over many years, all while caring for children sometimes with, and without, partners. The same would be true of the many black women in my family who would follow them, my mother included. But Elpernia's lot changed for the better when she arrived in Camden in the 1940s—at least temporarily.

Elpernia had saved her money, and she used it to purchase the home she later lost at 662 Randolph Street in East Camden. Learning my great-grandmother owned a home in Camden was instructive. Homeownership was a rarity among my immediate family. Most of my family members rented homes and apartments, as did the majority of the black residents in Camden. Those who owned would end up losing homes they had worked hard to purchase, like Elpernia. Years later, the home my mom's parents purchased in the Walt Whitman neighborhood of Camden was also lost after my grandfather, George, died in 2001.

A legal notice announcing a sheriff's sale of Elpernia's home was published in the local newspaper, the *Courier-Post*, on January 20, 1977, almost exactly a year after I was born. Dismayed, I reread the announcement several times. It was the only time Elpernia's name had been listed—not because of the good reasons I expected like a marriage announcement or a fantastic tale of a life crafted into a glowing obituary announcing her death in 1983, but because of the profound forfeiture of a home my great-grandmother worked hard to purchase. Hers was a tragic story of a flattened American dream.

The Federal National Mortgage Association stated that Elpernia owed $15,630.32 on her home. It is impossible to know the precise reason my great-grandmother fell so far behind in her payments or taxes. But it is no surprise she ended up losing her property. She was a black, working-poor woman living in Camden after its booming industrial mushroom had imploded. However hard she worked to keep up her payments, much was stacked against her, from the banks that refused mortgage loans to black buyers like her, to the speculators who took advantage of that lack to charge inflated prices for homes, to biased municipal property tax systems that charged more in black areas.

Knowing fair housing was not necessarily fair for everyone as a fact of history is one thing. It's something else entirely to discover that economic exploitation was the reason my family had to survive through poverty. My great-grandmother's loss was significant. The estimated $15,000 of negative equity she had accrued by 1977 is equal to about $61,000 today. Instead of building her wealth, her purchase of property sank her into debt. And there is no question that restrictions on where she could buy contributed to that tragedy. In my great-grandmother's case, as for so many other black Americans, the two were intertwined.

My great-grandmother's story is as much about the plight of black Americans in urban cities like Camden as it is a narrative of black survival amid deliberate repression. I needed to know how a black woman who taught herself to read and write, who at some point in her life managed to work sixty hours per week, care for children, and save money to purchase a home, ended up in the newspaper as the subject of a legal notice and not a story centered on audacious endurance. I needed to know how she had gone from owning a home to leasing a townhouse in a subsidized public housing development in Centerville. My great-grandmother's arrival in Centerville happened as the neighborhood was being strategically and securely contained as black, far before the projects were overly inundated with black and Latino residents who lived in inadequately built and mismanaged buildings. I only ever saw black residents walking along the narrow streets connecting the many public housing developments in Centerville. I didn't know white people were some of the first, and primary, residents of the rectangular-shaped brick buildings sprawled out across Centerville and other neighborhoods in Camden when segregated public housing was first introduced in the city in 1938. I needed to know why white people were imagined as bodies existing outside the bounds of public aid and housing. I needed to learn more about the expansive history of Camden and the ways black people were dispossessed of property, opportunities, and hope. I wanted to know more about the predominantly black city where so many of my family members and neighbors made do and thrived despite dispossession. This was the history untold in public schools I attended in Camden. It was history my family was aware of but did not talk about. Anyone who grew up in a city-turned-ghetto knows something about calculated calamity, even if it's hard to pinpoint the culprit. What I learned while writing this book are the reasons Camden became desperate in the first place.

TO CLAIM LOVE FOR a city so denigrated by the US media is to contradict every idea Camden residents have been socialized to accept. News reports during the first decade of the twenty-first century centered on 2000 US census data, which touted Camden as one of the poorest cities in the United States. Around the same time, Camden was also named the most dangerous city on a list generated by a widely criticized ranking compiled by Kansas-based Morgan Quitno Press, publisher of the annual "City Crime Rankings."

Far before experts began to crunch data in the early 2000s to validate others' assumptions about the mostly black city I learned to love, Camden residents were already used to being caricatured as spokes attached to a punctured wheel going nowhere quickly. We no longer lived in the "invincible city" Walt Whitman sermonized. Parts of our city smelled like shit. On October 27, 1980, the headline on the front page of the *Courier-Post* read, "In Camden, the Residents Live in Terror." The *Philadelphia Inquirer* published an article titled, "Violence, Delinquency Flare Among E. Camden Students" on March 10, 1985. According to the media, this was the Camden I was born into.

I loved the streets I grew up on despite the potholes, shells of buildings, and decay I was exposed to during my childhood. The many connected two-story brick row houses. The tiny homes that lined the corridors of alleyways. The community parks left deserted, and storied abandoned properties that reminded residents of a city that was once a booming center of commerce. Trash-lined corners, vacant lots, graffiti-tagged buildings, crack cocaine, and a downtown full of the ghosts of its former splendor. I loved them because they contained traces of our family histories and struggles.

The negative portrayals of Camden and the black people who lived there, which pointed to the problems that seemed to undermine any potential for good in Camden, always upheld the black and Latino inhabitants as the source of the violence and poverty plaguing the city. But that is a misguided and ahistorical idea. We were never the problem. The entrenched, interlocking systems of antiblack racism, economic disinvestment, and political exploitation ravaging Camden and its black and Latino residents were the sparks always smoking, and they preempted the eventual flames that would drastically shift the state of our city.

Camden was on fire in the summer of 1971. I was born into its aftermath five years later, in the winter, when it was still smoldering.

On July 30, 1971, Gerald E. Miller and Warren L. Worrell, two white patrolmen from the City of Camden Police Department, stopped forty-year old Horacio Jimenez (also known as Rafael Gonzalez). Horacio was talking to a younger friend when the officers demanded he return to his vehicle and move along. He complied, returned to his station wagon, and parked a block away on the corner of West and Benson Streets, where he continued his conversation.

The officers, both twenty-five years old, each stood nearly six feet tall and weighed about 190 pounds, according to an account published by the *Philadelphia Inquirer* on August 29. Horacio was six feet, four inches tall and weighed 200 pounds, but was cast as unnaturally large in the same article. "Jimenez is a big man, especially for a Puerto Rican," one reporter wrote, implying that he was freakishly large, innately brutish, and inhuman.

The officers approached Horacio on Benson Street and demanded he put his hands on the car. Reports from eyewitnesses tell an all-too-common story of police abuse in the United States. They beat him with nightsticks and fists. He was keeled over in pain when he was taken to the nearby Cooper Hospital. Shortly after his arrival, he was belted to a hospital bed after complaining about stomach pains. Bloodied, bruised, lacerated, and under police custody, Horacio fought to live despite his critical condition. No one knew at the time whether he would become a living reminder of the pervasive impact of police misconduct on the lives of black and Latino residents in Camden or a martyr for Puerto Rican liberation.

But Horacio was more than a symbol of institutional bias and disorder, liberation and justice. He was the husband of

Ruth Jimenez. Ruth and Horacio lived in a bungalow on a quiet street in Penns Grove, a suburban town about twenty minutes away from Camden, the city he once called home. He and his wife didn't have kids, but they kept chickens in their backyard. He had a family and was a construction worker.

He underwent surgery for a "rupture of the small bowel" and was treated for numerous cuts and bruises. He had a second operation on August 7 for "closure of wound breakdown." Horacio's deteriorating condition, and the pressure stemming from the public demonstrations led by Puerto Rican community leaders, were the reasons Miller and Worrell were charged with "atrocious assault and battery" on August 12. The officers were moved to "off-street" duty.

Horacio's condition did not improve. He suffered aspiration pneumonia, followed by heart failure connected to a general infection he developed from his wounds. He fell into a coma.

News of Horacio's worsening condition began to spread throughout the city. Puerto Rican residents, joined by their black comrades, began organizing. Residents rebelled against the city's silence. The Camden police reacted. The streets were covered in a fog of tear gas. Outnumbered police encountered infuriated and disheartened residents armed with bottles and rocks. Several buildings blazed across the city, including El Centro, the former church that was the main headquarters for Puerto Rican leaders. No one knows who started the fire. The local Woolworth's store downtown was looted, while other businesses, like the popular Broadway Eddie's record store, were left untouched because small red flags were hung outside, signaling solidarity with the Puerto Rican community.

My mother and her siblings lived with their parents a short distance from the center of most of the unrest, in the house on Woodland Avenue my grandparents would eventually purchase. My mom, who was eleven at the time, and her younger sister remember placing a red, black, and green unity flag on the outside of their home during the uprising, which lasted a few days. They remember the fear permeating their home and city, as well as the rage. They knew, too well, why it was necessary to fight back. My mom, aunts, and uncles, as black youth, were potential targets in a city where police abuse was common. Horacio's unresponsive body was a consequence of a state instrument working as it should, in the way that most law enforcement bodies do—functioning always as a tool of white supremacists' desires to protect white property and patrol nonwhite bodies. Black residents, like my mother's family, were intimately familiar with the injustices often brought upon them by those sworn to protect them.

In the upheaval that followed the Camden police officers' vicious assault on Horacio, some Camden residents burned parts of the downtown district to the ground. According to newspaper reports, Camden police shot 4 people and injured 87 more, and they arrested 144 people—the real number of those attacked and arrested by police could have been higher. Miller and Worrell were suspended from the police force on

August 21. Horacio remained in critical condition for six weeks before succumbing on September 15. His death was widely mourned among black and Puerto Rican residents. Around 10:30 a.m. the following day, Miller and Worrell turned themselves in. Their charges were upgraded to atrocious assault and battery and murder. A year later justice, as imagined by the community leaders who forced Mayor Joseph Nardi to respond to their seventeen demands the day the uprising began, had yet to be served. The acquittal of Officers Miller and Worrell in 1972 rocked the Puerto Rican and black communities. And the three nights of unrest, and its resulting destruction, continued a process of white flight already underway for three decades.

Uncovering the history of the 1971 uprising, after sitting with the heart-wrenching pain resulting from the deaths of so many nonwhite victims of police killings today, affirmed for me the truth so many of us know: black cities in the United States have always been on fire. There is nothing good that comes from hiding this truth. Had I read about Horacio Jimenez in the history books during my years in Camden Public Schools, or had my family told me about the muggy summer nights in 1971 when they placed solidarity flags outside their home, I might have understood why the streets I traveled were a phantom of a place once glorious or how our neighborhoods had become so blighted. I might have begun to understand why so many of the people I encountered in my classrooms and at bus stops seemed to carry the weight of hopelessness alongside profound, unrelenting courage. I would have not believed the lie that Camden had always been a ghetto, or that white people ran away because their once-industrious city had been destroyed by careless "niggers" and "spics." It would have been clear I had been brought up in a city crafted into a black ghetto by unseen hands, characterized as a site of violence and impossibility by past political leaders like Mayor Nardi, his police chief, the city's police force, and the media. I would have understood that the city once erupted because Latino and black residents were no longer willing to be crushed into neighborhoods too densely populated, enrolled in under-resourced schools, stuck in low-paying jobs, and living under a majority white law enforcement who saw them as bodies fit for extrajudicial liquidation. And to not re-tell, reclaim, and rewrite that history here would perpetuate the lie that the city I was born into was a hood simply because of the black and Latino working poor who live there.

I now split my time between New York City and Atlanta, but Camden is my home. Yet any home where some of the inhabitants are unwanted and neglected isn't much of a home at all. Black people had to be more than victims and sources of problems. I sensed as much growing up, but discovering the ways in which racial segregation, beyond redlining and housing discrimination, affected the lives of black residents in Camden was redemptive. Learning how the malicious unseen, but felt, forces of economic disinvestment, political deception, and cultural pathologization shaped my hometown helped to magnify the love I have for the city's people. It was proof that black families like mine had made a way despite the strategic forms of harm impacting their lives.

My grandmother once told me about the time she was driving alone in a suburb neighboring Camden in the late 1960s. When she stopped at a traffic light, three white men in the car next to her got out. She was terrified. The men each moved to a corner of her car and began rocking her car. She ensured her doors were locked, pressed her foot on the gas, and hit it. When I asked her what happened to the men, she responded by saying, "The hell if I know." Stories like my grandmother's were not uncommon among black people who lived in the Camden metropolitan area in the 1960s and 1970s. Stories of physical violence meted out by obvious racists are easy to name because they bear witness to the forces one can discern with clarity, but Camden has been shaped into the city it is today because of the various powers that were at work in stealth. And those are the stories that the broader public, beyond the people in Camden directly impacted, have yet to name.

The murder of Horacio Jimenez broke decades of silence regarding the violent discriminatory practices of local law enforcement in which the political establishment was complicit. It also animated the ongoing work of that generation's civil rights movement in Camden. Residents in my city were fighting on the frontlines in the same way freedom fighters were fighting in the South. Whether through small acts of solidarity like posting unity flags on the door, as my family did, or placing bodies in the way of bullets and tear gas, black people in Camden were not passive recipients of state violence and neglect.

The uprising of 1971 was more than an expression of rage at Officers Miller and Worrell. Puerto Rican and black residents refused to be sequestered in squalor and confined to the abyss of economic and political disempowerment. The absurdity of the history of racism, greed, and other forms of state-sanctioned inequity is its ability to reconstitute itself in the present. Camden burned in 1971. But the Camden uprising in 1971 is not widely discussed in history books like the civil disruptions in Los Angeles, Ferguson, Baltimore, or Chicago. Horacio's name does not appear among a litany of the dead like the names of Rodney King, Mike Brown Jr., Freddie Gray, or Rekia Boyd. The year was not 1991, 2014, or 2015. This was before white officer Darren Wilson shot and killed Mike Brown with impunity in Ferguson. This was before white officer Timothy Loehmann walked after fatally shooting twelve-year old Tamir Rice in a Cleveland park. This was before white officer Michael Slager, the Charleston police officer who was caught on video shooting unarmed Walter Scott as he ran away, walked after a jury of eleven white people and one black person could not unanimously decide on a verdict. This was Camden in 1971. My hometown. It marked the childhood of my mother's life and shaped the perceptions of the family I was born into.

My birth in 1976 occurred in the aftermath of one of the most significant events in Camden history. I sensed something had happened that turned our city into a place I would later attempt to run from, but recuperating the untold histories left out of my history books and family conversations has given me reason to return to the stories some may have been too ashamed to share, too burdened by to carry. I realized I could no longer forfeit the legacy I inherited while researching the histories of my family and hometown. Dispossession is not a secret we have to hold close because the city's slow death is not the fault of its black and Latino residents. And, really, there is no secret to hide when the insidious consequences of state neglect and greed continue to materialize and destroy the well-being of the people who call Camden home today. Those forms of repression are the hands that do their best work unseen. The hands we do not name but always sense moving among us that shaped Camden then, and continue to do so now. When we fail to bear witness to their presence, we aid in our own destruction. So I name them in this book. Camden is still alive because of its fearless people who wiggled their way out of premeditated suppression and, dare I say, the premeditated murder of their spirits. I am alive, today, because of the black family from Camden I was born into.

As a child, I walked past many fire-struck dilapidated buildings I was led to believe were burned down because of residents' inherent pathology and purposeful neglect, and not during a historical moment when a crushed people rebelled. I wasn't around to take in the smell of sulfur permeating our streets in 1971, but I would grow up wondering why the city I called home seemed to be in a state of constant recovery from hopelessness. I wanted to know why the ever-present funk in my neighborhood was so potent, and so ordinary, that its presence on Broadway seemed to create the perfect air for the crack cocaine epidemic, the burgeoning exploitative pimp industry, the sour economic residue of deindustrialization, and the political corruption that inundated Camden around the time I grew up. But I would later learn, as I came of age on Camden's streets, that hope often surfaces as the result of radical love. My family was my first example.

Chapter 2

RIPPLES

There were many nights I tried to skip bath time during my childhood. Even if my seven-year-old body smelled like "outside," as my mom would say, I would leap into my bed, without worry, smelling like a mix of grass, hot air, sweat, grime, and good times.

The bathtub in our small two-bedroom apartment felt too confining. And the way the water became sludge after I washed away the residue on my body left from hours of play repulsed me. I would move to the farthest end of any corner in the tub to avoid being touched by the once-fresh water made dirty after washing.

At some point, though, my dad decided he had had enough of my resistance. My dad loved the water. He swam with the grace of a bottlenose dolphin. When he went fishing, there was something about him that seemed to attract fish every time he released his pole. His brothers and sisters would tell me later that water was the element in which my father felt most disarmed and whole.

One evening after dinner, my father called me into the bathroom. As I walked closer, I could hear the water hitting the bathtub floor with force. The door was slightly ajar as he stood in the tub lathering a washcloth with Ivory soap.

"Open the door. What you standing there for?" he asked.

I walked into the bathroom with as much annoyance as I did whenever I needed to wash.

"I'm 'bout to teach you how to wash yourself properly. You can't be walking around here stinking. You getting older, and your body is changing," he said, and he prepared the washrag and soap as if we were about to begin a legitimate class on proper cleanliness.

I stepped cautiously into the steamy bathwater. It was the first time I stood in the presence of my father when he was naked, which actually made me forget about how much I hated washing. It was mystifying, to stand in the bathtub bare before the man who often veiled his deepest emotions and used the force of his physical power to dominate the spaces he moved through. I stared at him as he stood uncovered, more vulnerable and more self-possessed than I had ever seen him. He was twenty-three years old at the time, younger than I am now. But he was a father who was raising children. I can barely care for myself at forty-one, employed and relatively well paid, and cannot imagine all the tools he needed, and lacked, to properly care for my siblings and me.

"Get all the way in the water. Stop being scared. You gotta learn to clean your whole body, especially behind your ears and under your balls." He instructed me firmly, but with care and amusement, as we squeezed our bodies into the tub.

When we sat down, he moved his hand over mine. Together we grabbed the soapy washrag and moved it across my neck, behind my ears, along my arms, and across my chest.

My father gently washed my back as he instructed me on how best to clean the parts that smell the worst when boys play outside all day.

My fear of the bath dissipated more and more after each repetition of calm instruction offered amid safety in the presence of my father, who in other instances used the same hands to do damage. There was a lesson to be learned in the water. Bathing correctly was one lesson, but I also learned how tenderness and violence, care and harm, are strange bedfellows. They can coexist in our complex webs of human connection, the bad always canceling out the good, until the good that we are able to express smudges away the traces of evil even the best of us are prone to mete out. Looking back, I no longer see a young black father who was the totality of recklessness and lovelessness. I see a human being, a young black man, struggling to transform what he otherwise used as weapons into instruments of care. His hands, his strong and soft hands, were the source of contradiction in my youthful mind. His hands, his human and fragile hands, used gently and violently, now symbolize the complexity I too carry within and negotiate as an adult. In the water, we received instruction.

In her essay "The Site of Memory," Toni Morrison wrote, "All water has a perfect memory and is forever trying to get back to where it was. Writers are like that: remembering where we were, that valley we ran through, what the banks were like, the light that was there and the route back to our original place. It is emotional memory—what the nerves and the skin remember as well as how it appeared. And a rush of imagination is our 'flooding.'"

My mind is flooded with memories of a young father who tried his best to raise and protect the black boy he had at fifteen. I nearly drowned in Centerville Pool because of his commitment to ensure I learned to conquer water so it would not conquer me.

Centerville Pool was a central gathering place in Camden during the brutal northeastern summers. My cousins and I lived a short distance away in another neighborhood that was not teeming with housing projects, but that did not stop us from thinking any area full of the black poor, replete with unimaginative, densely populated two- and three-story housing units, like Centerville, was a ghetto despite my great-grandmother's presence there. Public housing was home to those black folks who were thought to dish out ass-whoopings with much more precision and expertise than everyone else.

My cousins and I traveled as a pack. My girl cousins would pull their coarse hair into tight ponytails, letting them rest upon their shimmering brown shoulders covered with towels. My scrawny legs would rustle against nylon swim trunks lined with white cotton mesh. As we made our way from Fairview to the pool, we joked about the filthy water we would soon leap into. We walked through the entranceway with caution, and we refused to walk on the pathway without flip-flops out of fear we would somehow contract herpes through our feet. We didn't realize our black bodies in the water figured as monstrous in some white racist's imaginings of blackness. We had been socialized to believe we were better because we lived in two-story row homes and apartment complexes with low rental costs and not the "projects," but we were the same as the black kids we swam with, full of joy and vitality, whose existences invalidated long-held racist claims of black inferiority.

One afternoon, my father arrived at the pool to swim. I panicked whenever my dad showed up in a public space full of my peers. There was no telling what he would do. If he overheard someone picking on me, I knew he would force me to retaliate with a punch. He also loved to brag about me. The son bragging made me just as uncomfortable, maybe more so. I suspected that others knew that Boo Boo's son wasn't as tough as he was. That day, however, he was set on making the two of us the center of attention.

My father was in the pool with his friends, all in their early twenties like him, and all full of youthful energy. They were swimming in the section of the pool where adults and Olympic-ready youth were allowed to swim. When my father wasn't around, I stayed in the beginner's section where I knew my feet could touch the bottom. My dad knew I could not swim and decided that day he would teach me to rule the water and my fears. He asked me to join him.

I timidly walked to the edge of the pool and hopped on his back. He whispered in my ear and let me know he was going to teach me. He didn't tell me the lesson would involve taking me out to the deepest end of the pool where he would perform a proper swim stroke with me on his back. In eight feet of water, he let me go. I sank and gasped for air while he tried to encourage me to copy his stroke. His directions were incomprehensible as I fought the water and tried to conquer embarrassment. The real, definitive boys and men stayed above the water and mastered the element that tried to control them. To sink, I thought, especially in front of your peers, was sissy shit.

My dad was intent on teaching me how to swim, but I wonder if he knew the real reason I avoided the pool. I hated going to the pool because I feared some of the neighborhood kids. Maybe he thought that his teachable moment would be a rite of passage—an expression of black masculinity that would assign me the privileges of hard-earned respect and protection on the streets. Perhaps he imagined my victory over the ferocious water would translate into the dissolution of so many of my other fears that provoked anxiety in me. Perhaps it was his way of quenching his own anxieties about my courage. Perhaps, this, to him, was an act of love and protection. If so, it was a strange love, but I sensed he wanted to protect and not harm me.

The love was deep, but its tides weren't so violent as to cause me to drown. It held me up, instead. And as I floated anxiously with my back atop its warm combers, I opened my eyes and stared at the expansive crystal blue hanging above my head as if it were the doorway into the heaven I was drifting through. I didn't want to return to the walkway. I wanted to stay close to his tender hands, so I stayed and drifted a bit longer, knowing the moment my feet once again touched the edges I would no longer be afraid to return to the water. Maybe it was another lesson to be discovered in the water, one that I would not recognize then but would understand later. Love, as James Baldwin admitted, is, indeed, a battle.

I remember the way I felt in those moments. The tight stitch holding together the love and fear I experienced in his presence also connected my heart to his. And in traveling back to the banks, the original place, where those feelings surfaced, I came across a valiant and complex black man standing on the shoreline inviting me to trust him to guide me gently into the water.

The more he talked, guided me, giggled as I squirmed, the more secure I felt about my body and his love for me. In the bathtub, he modeled a type of expressive and carnal bareness I've yet to experience with other black men in my life since. And in the pool, his presence marked security. With the black men I've encountered as strangers who became friends, uncles, and brothers, and the black men I've held close as we dreamt through nights in a bed we shared, impenetrable walls have kept us far enough apart to avoid the nakedness, so profoundly bare and safe, I experienced with the black man who taught me how to stay afloat in the water as a child.

THE WAY WE TALK about black teen parents, and growing up as a child of children in a black city, are two distinct forms of knowing. When I considered how hard it must have been to raise a child without the overwhelming support of family or the resources needed to care for oneself and a kid, I developed a deeper respect for the two young black parents who raised me.

My father was fifteen and my mother sixteen when I entered the world of the working-class black girl and boy who dropped out of school to care for me. My father dropped out of school after he completed eighth grade at Morgan Village Middle School. My mother, however, didn't have a choice. Her parents told her she needed to drop out to care for her child when she was in tenth grade at Camden High School. By the tenth grade, when I was the same age as my mother when she birthed me, I had already spent a few summers on the campuses of Rowan University and Camden County College as a participant in mathematics and science enrichment programs. And when I graduated from high school, I had already accumulated several college credits before I began my first year as an undergraduate. I knew nothing of the types of struggles my parents faced, which is why I've always been eager to learn more about them.

My father died suddenly while I was writing this book. I was emotionally debilitated for about two months and struggled to write with a broken heart. He was only fifty-five, and I didn't quite know the black man whose penetrating absence during parts of my life shaped the ways I love, or refuse love, and the work I do.

At his funeral, I tried my best to eulogize him. Had I finished writing this book before his death, these words would read differently. I would have written a slanted story depicting him as a monster, not the full human being I now know he was. As I write, I'm still awaiting return calls from family members who can tell me more about Grafton Harrity, the man behind the name, which still feels so unfamiliar and, yet, so memorable. He was buried along with his story and the answers to the many questions I had not asked him. What happened in his life that caused him to lose touch with the sweetness I had experienced during our interactions in my youth? What did it take to look me in the eyes as he held me in his small hands at fifteen? How did he manage to fall in love with my mom and fall so far away from the source of that love, compelling him to use his fists to keep her close? Why did he hide his love behind a hard exterior? Did he love us after she cried, after I screamed, before our relationship dissipated? Why did he disappear?

I buried a man I had known but knew little about. As is the case with most of my family members, our intimacy is as thick as the warm blood binding us, but we've learned to keep so much of our interior lives and secrets locked away. To truly know someone is to be fully aware of their inner lives, the people whose lives made their lives possible, and the context through which they have survived. There's much we don't know about each other. I learned a bit about my father, however, after he passed.

Before my birth, my dad played football against teams comprising neighborhood kids. As a boy, Boo Boo, as he was called, loved to cook and made his mother, Joyce Harrity, breakfast before he left the house to start the day at H. B. Wilson Elementary School, the same school my mom and I attended, in Fairview. He ate toasted bread covered in syrup and learned karate along with his younger brother, Bear. My father went to church sometimes, but the Gospel did not temper his love for trouble and juvenile antics. Once, in 1975, he and Bear found sacks of money their older brother, Perry, and sister's boyfriend, Buster, had stored in the house they lived in on Sylvan Street in Fairview. Bear recalls stealing the money and using it to buy outfits for school at E. J. Korvette's, one of several discount department stores owned by the chain, in the neighboring town of Audubon.

Boo Boo was named after his father, Grafton Dawson Wilson, a popular athlete in his own right whom peers at Glassboro High School called the "freight train." My dad wouldn't grow to be as big as his father, but he was just as popular for other reasons. He was known as a sharp dresser, and liked to wear tailored pants and shirts his mom purchased at Joe's Store on Kaighn's Avenue in Camden's Parkside neighborhood. And he was a prankster with caramel skin and impeccable swagger. But he was also caring. He joked a lot, but was also earnest. He did not allow my mother to starve, for instance, when they were childhood friends. His family had very little, but he gave a lot. He often brought her food when she was hungry because he cared for her. My mother was nearly raped once in the early 1970s and my father was the person who came to her aid. He slept in her backyard every night to protect her and was beat up by the perpetrator for it.

My mom was a beautiful black girl whom others recalled as reserved and mature. Her skin, smooth and brown like milk chocolate, never seemed to age. Her sisters described her as sneaky, an expert in getting herself out of trouble when necessary. She was modest, too. She always dressed neatly, and her hair was styled with precision at all times. She laughed boisterously sometimes, and when she did, her big bright smile would show her perfect white teeth.

I was mortified when I discovered as a child that a few of her pearly whites were fakes. One day she took them out. She slid them right out of the roof of her mouth as if they were part of an uncomplicated puzzle. I can't recall if I screamed or ran away, but she laughed at my shock. I felt bamboozled. It was the first moment when my mother, whom I thought was completely flawless, appeared imperfect. In my mind, until then, she was perfect.

Sixteen is an age when young people imagine futures, but my mom questioned whether she would build her own. She didn't see what was yet to come. My arrival paused time in my mother's life.

"It really didn't hit me," she recalled. "I was still doing normal things as if nothing happened until my friend told her mom and her mom told my dad. That's when all hell broke loose."

My mom was revered as a child. She cared for her six younger siblings, even though she too needed care. She made sure they ate and were prepared for school, properly dressed, and protected on the streets. Like so many black girls, she had less time to play than the black boys in her life. My father was still allowed to be a child, but my mother's childhood was cut short. The survival of my mom's siblings required her time and energy. She had already been mothering her siblings, but my grandfather punished her after he discovered she was pregnant.

"I got an ass beating out of my life," she told me.

Her answer stunned me. I loved, and lionized, my grandfather. She did as well. When I was a child, he was my strongest example of black manhood. Even when he failed, which seemed to happen less than often, I continued to love and accept him in ways I did not reserve love for my father when he faltered. When I asked her, years later, about the beginnings of male-perpetrated abuse in her life, I thought she would trace it back to my father, whom I would later love less. But she remembered the beatings handed to her by her father as the start of a routine pattern of domestic violence by the men she loved.

"My dad beat me until I pissed myself and was left lying in a puddle of urine. I was so scared. I didn't know what was going on."

Her plight wasn't unique. There are few geographies as fiercely desired and derided as the bodies of black girls and women. And my mother's body was no different. She was beaten because of the potential present within her being. Her pregnancy was a sign of her agency. Young black mamas, often represented as Jezebel figures, aren't glorified when they are actually seen as humans, or do as they will, or have sex for their own pleasure. My mom decided to give birth to a baby through a body she owned and was punished for it.

"I just said to myself, 'I'm having a baby. I'm so young. What are people going to say? How will I take care of a baby?'" She was mindful of her vanished years. Her questions weren't rhetorical.

My parents were among the 1 in 10 teenagers in the United States who had a child in 1976, a trend the *Los Angeles Times* reported in April of that year. The article described an epidemic of "pre-marital sex," "illegitimate births," and "births out of wedlock" as a social problem in need of prevention. My black body, a result of the intimacy shared between two black youths, was not illegitimate. My life was not worthless. The public hysteria sparked in response to teenage childbearing was unfounded. Black girls, the thinking went, were especially at risk of falling prey to this "epidemic." The pregnancy rate for unmarried black women was nearly seven times the rate for unmarried white women in 1970. The birthrate for unmarried white women has since steadily increased beyond the birthrate for unmarried black women. Yet black women still figure as the untenable problems in need of control.

The year I was born, Ronald Reagan railed against the infamous black "welfare queen" from Chicago who, according to him, "used 80 names, 30 addresses, 15 telephone numbers to collect food stamps, Social Security, veterans' benefits for four nonexistent deceased veteran husbands, as well as welfare" and whose "tax-free cash income alone has been running $150,000 a year." My teenage, unmarried black mother dropped out of school, lacked a diploma, was without substantive skills, and relied on government assistance to feed her family. Visits to the stark municipal building that housed the welfare office were common. She faced the shame coming from her parents at a moment when media, politicians, and the president-to-be made no secret of their contempt for poor and working-poor black girls and mothers like her. My mother was aware of her signification as a problem, but that did not stunt her drive to care for her children, even though she too was a child. The fact of her youthfulness, and the reality of the ways my birth shifted the direction of her life, never occurred to me. She was my mother, but to so many others her raising a child at a young age was a sign of irresponsibility. Strangers often mistook her for my big sister.

I attended kindergarten through third-grade classes at H. B. Wilson like my mom and dad. The school was outdated and colorless, and lacked individuality and innovation. The whiff of overheated, tasteless school lunches warmed up in industrial-sized ovens mixed with the stench of whole milk, all packaged in boxes, haunted the hallways like an evil spirit hell-bent on making me sick to my stomach.

Some of the desks and books were artifacts bearing the names of past students. Discovering my mom's scribbled signature in a tattered textbook in Mrs. Bank's first-grade class was either an indication my book was extremely old or that my mom's proximity to Mrs. Bank's resourcefully decorated classroom was closer than I had imagined. It was the first time I seriously pondered how close my mother and I were in age, but that one moment of clarity was followed by others.

Once my twenty-two-year-old mother stood on the sidewalk outside the old rectangular brick school building. She and several other mothers were waiting patiently as Mrs. Banks scolded the room of anxious, distraught first graders. She reprimanded us for bad behavior, and we were forced to stay an extra fifteen minutes after school as a result. Every minute felt like an hour, but our mothers said nothing, even after she went to the window and loudly informed them we were being punished for our actions. When I finally reached my mother, she let me know, "Mrs. Banks don't play. She did the same thing when I was in her class."

I was confused and tried to contemplate Mrs. Banks's age while imagining my mother twiddling her fingers on the top of one of the boxlike wood desks in that classroom. The truth was, my mother wasn't old. In fact, she was quite young. My teachers thought so, too, which is why some would often inform her that sisters of students could not sit in on parent-teacher conferences. She would let them know quickly, staring with her typical direct gaze, "I'm his mother." And that she was.

If I was a precocious boy child, it was because a derided black girl had raised me to be so, mostly in the absence of my father. I was never really surprised by the many moments I was told, or discovered, that my father was locked up in the county jail or one of New Jersey's adult correctional institutions. I was unbothered by his lack of presence during my childhood. And I expected that letters from my dad addressed from strange places with a series of numbers placed slightly below his name would one day land in our mailbox. In the letter, we would learn what correctional institution he was in, his needs, and other family members or friends he happened to run into while there. The institutions supposedly designed to correct my father failed, almost expertly. He returned many times after the first.

My father was in and out of jail throughout his adult years. The late 1970s and early 1980s was a moment when the lives of black people were negatively impacted by policies emerging during the Reagan era, from mandatory sentencing to the "war on drugs." In the late 1980s, families of incarcerated persons, like us, were used to signing up for free transportation to and from correctional facilities. My mother would dress my three younger sisters and me in our best clothes, prepare and bag lunches, and place toiletries and other treats that were to be given to my father in clear Ziploc bags. Everything was checked before boarding, including us. We would take a public transit bus to Camden City Hall, which doubled as the city's short-term jail, where we would then wait with other families, all black and Latino, all working poor, to board a yellow or blue bus that would take us on our journey to places like the East Jersey State Prison in Rahway. At the time, East Jersey State seemed to be many worlds away from Camden.

I felt ashamed during our visits. The body and bag checks, the guarded buses with tinted windows, the many instructions to be followed from the time we waited in line to board the bus until we were allowed time with our incarcerated family members—all were embarrassing, and strategic, lessons. The visits were designed to teach us, black and Latino family members traveling along the ghetto-to-prison pathway, how to be proper citizens, different from the shady criminals we were granted free transportation to visit. Unbeknownst to me at the time, the correctional institutions we visited in mostly rural and suburban areas of the state bolstered the economies of predominantly white towns, thanks to the ever-increasing population of incarcerated black and Latino fathers, mothers, daughters, and sons.

Back in Camden, and without the help of my father, my mother cooked for us, managed our home, paid the electric bill, purchased and washed our clothes, made sure we were groomed, reviewed our homework, scolded us, and cared for us after leaving an eight-hour shift where she would unload boxes of products from trucks that she then stacked on the shelves of Bradlee's Department Store in Audubon. She carried the double burden of mothering her kids and my father as if we were all her children. I could not see the invisible weights she carried because she did what she could to lessen our load as children growing up without the daily presence of a father.

His absence only amplified her presence. And her presence brought me complete joy.

I was my mother's little boy, and the child her siblings helped raise. My aunt Barbara, for example, was a tenth-grade student and participant in Camden High School's childcare preparation program. I was one of her students. She walked to school with her book bag and nephew in tow. That is just one example of the ever-present type of care provided in our home. It flowed from every direction. And that is why the realities of economic struggle weren't as noticeable to me as a child. I never went a day without eating or worried about having a place to lay my head because I had been raised by black people who would sooner welcome another, whether family member or friend, they were angry with than leave them on the streets to suffer. No one person was left to struggle alone.

My mom and her siblings exemplified the true meaning of family. They argued and forgave. They were temporary enemies during certain stages of their lives, and they were lifelines during times of need. Lack didn't impede their ability to care for one another; it made care possible. Their example taught me why it was, and is, necessary to reject stereotypes about black people without wealth. They were rich in empathy, support, and compassion. Had we been born into money I believe we would have revered things, our material possessions, and our individual selves, the false gods of American capitalism, and not the people we snuggled up next to in twin-sized beds or on living room floors. That powerful form of connection is what critics of Camden missed. People who lived outside our city ostensibly saw only the social problems that were present on the surface, but they failed to understand and take into account the fundamental, everyday ways in which black families like mine demonstrated care within our homes even when care was not extended from city hall, police headquarters, and the governor's office.

Care does not look like police patrolling blighted neighborhoods in search of people who fit the description of the assumed criminal, to fill up jail cells and meet quotas, both built on the false premise that black people are more prone to violence. Instead, care looks like neighbors passionately intervening to ensure the safety of people they know, and strangers they don't, who have been assailed by police, many times for no reason other than the color of their skin. I observed many interventions as a youth. Care—the kind of support that one gives to push another toward wholeness—is not a consequence of apathy. Welfare legislation designed to redeem the poor, whom most people assume loathe working and rely on the state for handouts, is not about care if it isn't grounded in the truth that our American economic system has always purposefully favored the rich. Care is my aunt Arlene stealing food, mindful of the consequences if she were to be caught, so her sisters' and brothers' bellies could be a bit more full when they lay down in their beds to rest. My family cared deeply in the absence of polices and programs that were grounded in love. As a child, I assumed the world was full of people just like them who loved just as hard and sacrificed just as much.

That is why I played more than I worried as a child. It's why I smiled more than I frowned. It's what made me remember the good nights before the bad mornings. My mom and her people protected me from the truth and taught me that the world outside our door, a short distance away from home, a world inhabited by white people and black people with money, may not be as hospitable. But I would also learn that the safest spaces, like our homes, can be just as hostile.

MY PARENTS RENTED THEIR first two-bedroom flat in Crestfair Apartments when I was about nine years old. After my mom left her parents' house on Broadway, she moved in with my father's sister, Aunt Cookie, who lived in a house with her two kids on Sylvan Street in Fairview, before she and my father moved to Crestfair. One evening after playing, I walked onto the cement entryway connecting our small two-bedroom apartment to the two others our home was nestled between. I thought twice about opening the rickety white screen door because I heard the sound of my mother's loud sobbing and my father's voice blasting. Up until then, I had never heard or seen my mother cry. My father was never that loud and unruly unless he was cracking jokes or singing along with the Temptations or the Whispers in his tenor squeal.

The lights were on when I entered. My mom's upper body was sprawled across our beige couch. Her face was wet with tears. She stared at me through her drowning eyes, as my father bent one of her arms behind her back with force, as he pounded the back of her body. She looked at me as if she wanted to me look away, but I was stuck in place. My father's eyes were red and glassy. His lips quivered as he threatened her. "I will fuck you up! You hear?"

His hands were no longer tender as they had been with me, but were now used as weapons to make my mom submit. And my presence did not seem to matter. He only beat her more after I hurried to my room. I covered my head with my pillow to escape the noise. That was the first of many scenes of domestic abuse I would witness.

Christmas was a holiday when my mom did all she could to create a fantasy in the midst of chaotic struggle. She would purchase gifts clandestinely when they were on sale at Bradlees and hide them in the basement of the two-bedroom row house we moved into in Polack Town, after we left Crestfair.

I didn't sleep through the night, like many kids, on Christmas Eve because excitement would keep me awake. I could not wait to put my hands around the He-Man and GI Joe figurines I'd use to battle Optimus Prime. One Christmas Eve, when I was twelve, my mom asked me to help her wrap gifts. I was Santa's helper. Santa was a twenty-eight-year-old, minimum-wage-making, government-subsidy-supported black mother from Camden, and not a rotund, bearded white man from the North Pole. I was proud to be invited to do what the adults in my family had done years before and help create an atmosphere of surprise and happiness for my three younger sisters, Latasha, Tamisha, and Sekeena.

My mom and I carried boxes filled with Cabbage Patch Kids, board games, Barbie doll cars, and clothes from the basement to our living room. We cut huge swaths of wrapping paper and used them to cover each gift with care, taping bows on and fastening labels bearing Santa's name—some were labeled "Mom" and some were labeled "Dad" even though my mom had purchased them all. The mood was celebratory and nostalgic as we listened to the mix of old and new Christmas songs on the radio. When my father arrived home with one of his friends, the serene bonding moment my mother and I shared was interrupted.

"What the fuck is all of this?" my dad asked as he looked over all the boxes we'd placed under our synthetic tree.

"They're the kids' gifts." My mother seemed used to my father's direct questioning. She continued to pile the gifts under the tree as if she didn't sense the tension sucking the joy out of the atmosphere.

Within seconds of her reply, my father threw her to the ground and started to beat her in front of his friend and me. The Temptations' rendition of "Silent Night" was drowned out by yelling and the sounds of punches. I ran to the phone and called my grandparents' house. My aunts, uncles, and grandparents lived a short walking distance away.

"Hello?" a voice on the other end of the phone said.

"We need help. Please come over. My dad is beating my mom. Please come." It was the first time I called for help and probably the first time my aunts were clued in on what had been hidden from them for a few years. My aunt Barbara showed up at our house frazzled. My father, and the black male friend who watched as he threw my mother across the room, left before she arrived.

"Are you okay?" Barbara asked.

My mom told my aunt she was all right and that it was okay for her to go home. The house was silent again until my mom called to me from the top of the stairwell. She was enraged. She ran down the steps, grabbed me, and beat me with her hands as she yelled, almost through tears, "Whatever happens in this house stays in this house. You hear me?"

A few years before I started writing this book, she apologized. She told me she was sorry for her response in a moment when the only emotions she could feel were embarrassment and anger. For so long, I resented her for beating me because I had tried to help. But I understand now. She had done all she could to disprove her parents' belief that she and her kids wouldn't be shit. Finding out she was living with a man who beat her would only prove them right.

During my teens, these scenes of beatings replayed in my mind like a series of old sitcoms. Holding onto painful secrets feeds on the heart like a cancer. Every attempt at blocking out the memories, every act committed to anesthetize the pain, was useless. When I was twelve, I threatened to jump from the bedroom window in our house. My sisters cried out for me to stop. In school, I poured every ounce of energy I possessed into my schoolwork and after-school activities. At home, I got lost in my dreams and fantasized about a life without a woman-beating father. And on the streets, I slowly took on a hard demeanor, losing smiles and compassion, vowing to hurt anyone before they hurt me. The only way cancers can be stopped is by acknowledging their existence and doing what you can to treat them. And sometimes relief comes when the source of the problem is removed.

The last time I saw my father before losing contact with him for several years, he had just finished breaking the glass pane in our backdoor. I was thirteen. It was a late winter afternoon and the sky was overcast. A short time before, my father had come by our house with the same friend who was with him on Christmas Eve, and together they left with my youngest sister Sekeena. She was five years old at the time. She wasn't with them when they returned. My dad stood on our front porch, where he told his friend, "I'm gonna kill her." He tried, unsuccessfully, to get in through the front door. His friend stayed close to his car that was running in the front of the house while my father made his way to the backyard.

My mom was visibly shaken and my sisters and I were scared as we watched him place his hand on the knob to open the door. I prayed for his plan to fail, but he got in by breaking the glass pane and reaching in. He tossed my mom across the kitchen floor. He punched her and then opened the oven door where he positioned her head. And he kicked and kicked and kicked her arms, legs, and head with his feet. He was wearing black construction boots.

"Get off of her!" I yelled. My father turned to me, looked me in the eyes, and seemed more hurt and surprised than angry. The words had traveled from the deepest pit of my stomach and out of my mouth. I was as stunned as he was. But I refused to stay silent any longer.

"Oh, you bad? What you gon' do?" he asked. And then he hit me.

That was the first time my father had used his hands to hurt me. The hands that had only ever held me with tenderness, he used now to break my spirit and bruise my mother's face. I gave up whatever love I had for him in that very moment.

My aunts and grandfather George eventually showed up. Aunt Arlene, my mom's younger sister who was known as the family protector, held my mom close and promised she would be okay. Boo Boo was arrested that day after Aunt Arlene beat him until he was unconscious and stretched out on the floor of our porch. My grandfather ran down the street with a hammer he swung at my dad's friend. He demanded they travel together to get Sekeena from wherever she had been left. Mom was safe. Sekeena was found and returned. And my father was locked up. I felt a strange sense of relief and happiness. I was also broken. My relationship with my father would never be the same.

JANUARY 15 IS A day full of complexity. Every celebration of Martin Luther King Jr.'s birth is another opportunity to highlight the type of college-educated, Christian, married, suit-wearing, and respectable black man society deems worthy of public praise. My father was born in 1961, on the same day as King but thirty years later. Two black men, one an American hero and the other its proverbial nightmare.

America is obsessed with images of the good black man whom niggas should strive to emulate. Forget King's own internal and private conflicts made public by J. Edgar Hoover's FBI. Marital infidelity and imperfections aside, the respect reserved for King has much to do with America's fascination with black men it regards as great, even when those same men have been demonized and killed before their deification. America's relationship with King since his death has been a one-sided love story centered on a man made out to be less human and complex than he actually was. I compared my father to King. My father, I thought then, was less great. But that is not what I think today, as I write and remember his humanity.

Boo Boo was a black boy who may have dreamt about a life full of promise, resources, respect, and familial love. But how much of a life, free of troubles and self-detestation, can a fifteen-year-old boy concerned with raising an infant build before his sense of self is devoured? How could he withstand the effects of immense poverty, lack of education, lovelessness outside of his home, restrictive rules governing the code of thuggish black manhood he performed, quests for internal power to upset the reality of material disempowerment, the lure of the street, and the force of white America's fear-induced policing of his body? I don't have any answers, but I imagine the many societal expectations he tried to meet were only magnified by the presence of a woman partner who succeeded where he had seemingly failed. In no way is this an excuse for his bad decisions, absence, and abuse. But it is a reckoning with the lived experiences of a black boy who had trouble loving his best friend and their children because he had no sense of the tenderness within him or not enough faith in the love and hope we had for him.

My mother discovered her strength because she had no choice but to do so. She survived the violence inflicted on her body and psyche by the black men she loved and celebrated after they hurt her. Her kids, she told me years later, were the reason she fought so hard to live. I wanted her, however, to live and fight hard for herself. In many ways she has. It took years, until she was fifty, but she eventually earned her high school diploma. That day was one of the proudest moments of my life.

I buried a man who was stuck. He was forever attempting to break away from the world of the black boy who didn't finish grade eight, the one who had a kid at fifteen, a boy who was pulled in by the lure of the streets, a teen who would later beat the girl he got beat up for protecting, a black man frozen in time. He was a black man who swung back when love sometimes showed up in the form of an embrace. We are the same. Like my father, and so many other black men, some of us don't really ask for what we want because to ask for love is to ask for what has been denied us for so long. How many of us want what we have been told we cannot, or are not allowed to, have? Interpersonal and structural forces shape the ways we give and receive love as well as the violence we men sometimes inflict upon our partners. I am not sure if that was his struggle. I know it is mine, largely because of his absence, which is a truth I believe had weighed him down.

The last words I spoke over his unconscious body as he rested on a hospital bed, surrounded by the kids he had left long before, were simple: "Fly. I know you are heavy. We forgive you. Whatever weights you have been carrying, let them go. Fly."

I only told him what I learned to do in his absence.

Chapter 3

MAGIC

The dog-eared textbooks weighed down my backpack as I marched from my classroom to my guidance counselor's office at Morgan Village Middle School, which was a cluster of beige brick circular buildings connected by a dizzying array of carpeted hallways. My mind spun as I walked the annulus, focused on the one charge emboldening me that late winter day. I was determined to not leave my guidance counselor's office until my demands were met. Having already completed two years at Morgan Village with much success, I wanted to know why it was a few of my closest friends had been pulled out of our classes during our Language Arts and Social Studies blocs while the rest of us remained behind.

Each semester, I placed dark yellow report cards, brimming with A's handwritten in blue ink, in my mother's hands with pride. When I received the results from the California Test of Basic Skills (CTBS), an assessment required of all eighth-grade students in Camden Public Schools in the early 1990s, I was more determined than furious and more furious than ecstatic. My grade equivalency was ranked at 12.9, which meant I tested at the same level as the majority of students who were in their nine month of twelfth grade, even though I was only in eighth grade. But I felt I had nothing to show for it. Unlike my friends, I did not get to pack up newer and more expensive-looking books when the bell shrieked, signaling it was time to leave overcrowded classes behind. I envied them and looked down on myself. But indignation and pride can be a potent blend in the mind of a fourteen-year-old black boy whose source of power is his dreams. My dad never finished his eighth-grade year at the same school. I was determined to not only finish, but to do so magnificently.

"Can I talk to Ms. Yeldell?" I asked the administrative assistant.

She always guarded the guidance and principal's offices as if any request for a meeting was an assault on her personally. For once, though, she didn't ask any questions. After Ms. Yeldell was summoned, she came out of her office dressed as opulently as ever in a light-colored dress and dark blazer, ornamented with jewelry. Her wavy black hair was pulled back from a face that was brown and chiseled. I followed Ms. Yeldell into her office while I replayed my explanation for the meeting as if I were memorizing a script.

"What do you want to talk about?" she asked as she stared directly into my eyes. I handed her copies of my CTBS scores and report cards.

"I want to know why I'm not in AT."

AT was shorthand for classes for the "academically talented." It was the designation teachers and students used to refer to the classes my friends were pulled out to attend. AT was an enchanted place in my mind—a place where students had spirited discussions, and where the far-off worlds we explored in books came alive and the most complex mysteries were solved. It had to be a special place if only a few of my classmates were granted entrance.

My friends Richard and Lawrence would return to classes packed with more than two-dozen uninterested students after spending their time in AT. I would stare them down with a look of exasperation because I sensed our diverging educational experiences were based on a set of different expectations, despite our placement in the same school.

The problem, however, was more complex and vast than my own grievances.

The Camden City School District was failing its students. Like most schools located in economically devastated places in the United States, Camden's formula for per pupil education was based on the city's depleted property tax base. There could be a neighborhood in which people owned decrepit old houses and there still wasn't enough money for new textbooks because property taxes were so low, which meant the food thrown onto our trays during lunch and the courses we had access to were limited as a consequence of poverty. In 1990, the statewide average for per pupil spending was $5,000. Schools in Camden received $4,000 per student, while suburban towns in New Jersey received substantially more. Cherry Hill, for example, spent over $6,000 per student, and Princeton spent over $8,000. Wealth granted access to shiny new textbooks, computers, classes with fewer students, after-school activities, additional counseling support, and all of the charmed supplements my peers in AT were provided. But securing resources for the small group of students considered gifted meant the majority of the 19,000 young people who were students in Camden Public Schools in 1990 would receive close to nothing.

While I was a student, the state of New Jersey was forced to recognize that its public education system willfully disadvantaged those of us who lived in poor urban districts. This was in 1990—nearly two decades after the New Jersey Supreme Court had ruled the per pupil funding formula was unconstitutional because it relied too heavily on property taxes. I was fully aware of all of the resources the schools I attended lacked, but I didn't know there were legal and political fights taking place on behalf of my peers and me at the time.

The Education Law Center, a legal advocacy organization based in Newark, New Jersey, and established by a Rutgers University law professor named Paul Tractenberg I would coincidentally work with in my mid-thirties, filed a series of monumental lawsuits that caused the state to drastically change its funding formula. The legal battles, the most critical of which were the *Abbott v. Burke* decisions, began in 1981 and were still going on in 2017. In May 1990, Governor James Florio introduced the Quality Education Act, which would increase the budgets of thirty-one "special needs" urban districts in the state in response to *Abbott v. Burke II*. Camden was one and was set to receive a budget increase of $50.6 million to address the problems summarized in Jonathan Kozol's damning 1991 book *Savage Inequalities: Children in America's Schools*, which explored the disparities impacting districts in economically devastated cities like East Saint Louis, Washington, DC, and Camden. The increase may have seemed impressive, but the proposed amount would only help the district manage some of its long-standing inadequacies if granted. Uplifting the spirit of Camden public schoolteachers and students was not a dilemma money could solve alone.

A *Courier-Post* article titled "Report Condemns Lack of Resources" was published on December 23, 1990. I had graduated from Morgan Village by the time of its publication, but its findings were entirely consistent with my experiences while in Camden public schools. In 1990, the dropout rate was 10.8 percent, students were scoring below the national average on college entrance exams, facilities were overcrowded, staffing was described as inadequate, instruction time was insufficient, elementary schools lacked libraries and library technologies, the district lacked computers, students did not have much access to fine arts and music courses, and the district suffered from a lack of instructional resources. My adolescent intuition was apparently more precise than I realized at the time. It would take seven additional years, however, before the New Jersey Supreme Court's ruling in *Abbott v. Burke IV* ordered state officials to immediately increase funding for urban schools so that there could be parity between them and schools in the suburbs.

My small battle with Ms. Yeldell, however, scored me a win much sooner than the state's Supreme Court. I can still recall the look of surprise on Ms. Yeldell's face as she shifted her gaze from my test scores and report cards to my unyielding face. "I see. I didn't realize you scored so well. Let me see what I can do."

The next day when the bell rang, I packed my bags with anticipation. Ms. Yeldell came to my class with a transfer slip prepared for my teacher. She accompanied me to the room where I had imagined learning as a process more glorious and advanced than what I was experiencing. When I entered, a stern-faced white woman was sitting at the front of the room behind a desk covered neatly with books. Ms. Compo was one of a few white teachers I had during the first eight years of my schooling in Camden, and was seemingly the teacher deemed most fit to educate the small collection of black special students.

Richard, Lawrence, and a few other students sat at pristine desks positioned neatly before Ms. Compo. Colorful maps boasting cartographies of an expansive world beyond New Jersey were posted on the walls. The room lacked the noise of the jokes and juvenile banter that disrupted the calm in so many of my other classes. And there were many books— novels of various lengths, colorful resource materials, and new textbooks. Ms. Compo had demanded we neatly cover the exterior of every book with brown paper bags. It was a routine we followed to keep our books in good shape. Any student who failed to follow her orders would have points deducted from his or her grade.

Every night, including weekends, I now had dozens of pages of literature to read—*Of Mice and Men, 1984, Romeo and Juliet,* and *Animal Farm*—but I would not fail. I had worked hard to prove I was worthy of the place I scored among the academically talented and wanted to be sure Ms. Yeldell and Ms. Compo didn't doubt it. Unfortunately, my individual ascension would be of no consequence for all of my peers who still had to return to the overcrowded classes I left. And while the better story would be one where I am portrayed as an exception, a student more worthy of better schooling than others, I was no more gifted than they were. I was a resourceful and determined teen, but every student at Morgan Village deserved to read from books our parents' names were not scribbled in. The failure of the state to make good on its constitutional commitment to provide a quality education to every child was the problem, but I didn't fully realize then how the mechanics of purposeful disenfranchisement worked. At fourteen, I figured I had beaten the system. I had won.

The special trips we took were only part of the consolation prize for winning the fight. I experienced my first multicourse meal, complete with appetizers and multiple utensils, for example, at a Chinese restaurant in a neighboring suburb. Ms. Compo wanted us to experience different cultures, but I was ashamed because I didn't know the difference between the forks assembled before us. I wasn't the only person surprised by my achievement. Ms. Yeldell was beaming with pride during my eighth-grade graduation. I received a few honors, including the highest award for achievement in social studies despite having been a part of the exclusive world of AT for only two semesters. "I am so proud of you," Ms. Yeldell repeated. I had to prove to her I was deserving of the opportunity, and I succeeded in doing so.

The emotional pain I suffered growing up produced a dogged strength. It also sparked my imagination. And I wonder if others saw that spark in me. For so long I thought bullies latched onto what they perceived as my weaknesses, but what if they were really attracted to the courage I had yet to realize I possessed? Waking up almost daily with puffy eyes because I fought sleep the night before out of fear my mom could be killed by the time I woke up. Returning to the same streets I sprinted across day after day while being chased by schoolmates who seemed to enjoy the pursuit. Every time I returned to the classroom or cafeteria despite the fear of taunts from students like James from Centerville and OB from Polack Town, two teens who seemed to be drawn to and repulsed by my presence, signified an internal force pushing me forward.

When I left my house every morning, I knew I would have to employ the power within my grasp to survive potential danger. But sometimes there aren't any spaces where we can be safe. In those instances, we learn to protect ourselves; we learn to build forts. Wands and incantations, ingenuity and prayers, however, were more useful than fists and insults at fourteen. I won the fight against annihilation, by my hands and those of others, by losing myself in my dreams. In my dreams, I mapped out the routes I would need to abscond. Every danger presented another opportunity to quicken my speed when violence was imminent. Difference is often the calculus for such violence, but the unexplainable strength within us sometimes safeguards us from its grip. Dreams die if they are consigned to the imagination only. They are the seeds we must be able to plant in the outside world; at least, that is what I now know, having remembered the ways I manifested dreams as a youth.

At forty-one, I still look back to the strong-willed person I was as a child. Whenever I feel as if I can't leap over a hurdle, whenever I am scared to go after what I want, whenever I am paralyzed by fear and shame, I remember the young black boy who dreamt aspirations into existence. Dreams are the destinations we arrive at as we chase our wishes and our callings. I learned to run, not away from bullies, but in pursuit of the passions that enflamed my heart. I was a persistent and resilient black boy—despite the forces that attempted to stop me from pursuing my dreams and the forces that tried to end my life during the pursuit.

I EXPECTED BANTER. I wasn't prepared for a beating.

Fuji, OB, Mark, and another boy whose name I did not know were hanging out on my next-door neighbor Mark's porch, watching me as I walked home from the corner store with my grandma's daily regimen of fifty peppermints and a *Courier-Post*. My mother, my three sisters, and I had moved into our grandparents' home in the Whitman Park neighborhood in Camden in 1990. We had to relocate because our home five minutes away had been destroyed by my mom's boyfriend, Charles. My grandparents lived on a densely populated street full of small, differently colored, and attached row houses. Some of the homes were boarded up and abandoned, a few were well manicured, and others had been knocked down, leaving behind vacant lots. A few of the corners in our neighborhood were populated with black boys, and some girls, who found community where police found reason to stop and frisk us. Others sold drugs and were gang members. I was excited about the move and wasn't bothered that every night my mom and I slept on the two couches opposite one another in the living room of the packed family house. I would close my eyes knowing my mom was safe.

Our street was usually tranquil in the late spring, especially after school. The hot sunlight would shimmer on the tiny glass shards left from broken bottles on the cement sidewalk. The neighborhood kids would be inside acting as if we were doing homework, or playing games on our Nintendo or Sega systems, while our caregivers made their way back to homes full of people, problems, love, and concern. Even the fearless street pigeons, fiercer than any stray dog that chased passersby for fun, seemed to be reserved that day.

"Why you such a fucking faggot?" OB, the oldest and toughest of the crew, asked as he uncoiled the plastic cap covering the milk jug he held in his hand. The boys walked toward me and surrounded me before I was able to make it home.

OB's taunts were routine. By fourteen, I had perfected the art of indifference. Slurs like "gay" and "pussy" would be met with a giggle and smirk as if they did not cut. My smile was fraudulent. I held back tears and swallowed the stinging embarrassment.

"Faggot!"

My heart started racing. I was standing a few feet away from my grandparents' house, but the boys were blocking my movement on the sidewalk.

The uncovered milk carton was nearly full, but I realized it didn't contain milk. I could smell gasoline, and I wondered if it had come from the small yellow moped my uncle had given me. My bike had been stolen several days before. The rumor circulating on the block was that OB had taken it. I was actually relieved when it disappeared because I was too scared to take it for a ride.

"You scared, pussy? What you gonna do?" OB asked.

I didn't have a response. I never did when he or anyone else hurled insults. This time, however, I sensed OB wanted to do more than taunt me. OB started pouring the gasoline on me, but before he could finish I pushed him away. I was thin and lacked definition. OB was fit. I only shoved him to keep him from hurting me. I was too frightened and caged in by their bodies to inflict harm. OB was pissed.

Within seconds, he had emptied the gasoline on my head. The liquid covered my body. I could barely see. My eyes were glazed and throbbing. The pungent smell of fuel, which belonged in a moped tank and not a child's mouth, heightened my senses. The block was eerily silent. The wind seemed to have stopped whistling. The cars blazing loud rap songs on woofer speakers seemed to disappear. I was dazed.

I felt hands—many hands—violently hammering my body.

I caught a few glimpses of OB as he attempted to strike the match. It flickered several times. However, the wind instinctively seemed to put out each flame. And he grew even angrier. His handsome caramel-brown face lost its look of youthful innocence. His forehead was furrowed and his eyes were slightly squinted. He looked disappointed. He seemed defeated because he could not light the match. He was unable to watch me burn.

I was in shock and emotionally numb. The psychic pain was so deep I could no longer sense its presence. I barely remembered Mark, Fuji, and the stranger were ever there. I was focused on OB and the matches in his hand. And death felt close.

My aunt Barbara happened to be walking home and saw the boys pounding me. She intervened swiftly. She was a well-dressed young woman with mocha-brown skin. Her five-foot-seven frame was petite, but she has always been full of courage and, as my mom would say, "a lot of mouth." Family members made fun of her. They called her "skinny" and "bones." That day "bones" saved my life just as she and her sisters saved my mom's.

Aunt Barbara held me with one hand as she swung the other. Her fists landed on the bodies of the boys with force. They scattered and she cussed. "Leave him the hell alone! Fucking punks!" They snickered as she screamed.

She gathered my things and walked me to what was then named West Jersey Hospital, about ten minutes away from our home. We had a big family, but no one living at my grandparents' house had a car at the time, so we took New Jersey Transit buses or walked to get around. That day was no different.

Aunt Barbara held my small hand as I stumbled forward, with gasoline in my eyes and on my skin. I cried uncontrollably when they cleansed my eyes with water. I sat in a triage room wearing a tight plastic hospital patient bracelet around my wrist and a thin blanket wrapped around my upper body. I thought about how pathetic I looked.

Why did I have to be the weak boy in the family? With my shuddering eyes and a loose wrist, why was I different? Why was I less rough than Mark and OB, always in need of a protector, too smart, too much of a geek, too feminine? Why me?

I asked myself those questions as I sat on the couch, once I was back at home. The feeling of embarrassment was as overpowering as the bitter smell of the gas that emanated from my body. The penetrating smell and astringent taste of gas are unforgettable. On bodies it gives the impression death is near. The ER doctor had instructed Aunt Barbara to keep me covered with a blanket out of concern I might be flammable still. There I sat humiliated, on the couch in front of my mother, a few aunts, my grandmother, two uncles, three younger sisters, and cousins.

"They need their asses beat," one of my aunts said, interrupting the tense silence.

My mother was livid. "Get up!" she ordered.

I reluctantly followed her. She marched me to two of the four boys' homes. Mark's first, since he lived next door. Fuji's second, because he lived around the corner.

She knocked on each door, fists landing like a hammer. She didn't tell me she was fed up with my beatings, but I sensed the hurt and exhaustion in her voice. She looked at me sternly while cautioning Fuji's mother, "I should make my son whoop his ass!" I relaxed my chest and swallowed the fear that was lodged in my throat. Fuji tried to push past his mother and make his way through the door to fight with me. His mother held him back. They had apologized to my mom, but they didn't look remorseful. They looked at me with pity as I slowly maneuvered farther away from Fuji's reach. I wasn't like the other boys in my neighborhood. I wasn't like the girls in my family, either. The girls would fight the boys in my neighborhood without hesitation or fear. Sometimes they would fight for me. I was too tired and scared to be beaten twice in one day.

All these years later, I still don't understand what would provoke OB. What made him so angry he would want to kill me? I knew little about his family and personal life, but I knew enough. I knew the immense poverty he and his siblings endured, and I knew that the violence that had become mundane in our neighborhood had begun to shape him in the same ways it had started to shape me. I shed fewer and fewer tears every time I was told another young person had been murdered in my neighborhood. People died often. Maybe OB and I were more alike than I wanted to believe.

I also bullied some of my peers. In middle school, I joked about Richard's body and his grown-folk smell. He was not an average-sized fourteen-year-old. I called him "fat" and "stinky" as our classmates chuckled. And whenever my neighbor Jamal would walk by my aunt's house when I was in high school, I would loudly start listing the alphabet out of order or whisper "yellow bus" just loud enough that he could hear me. Jamal was in "special education" classes.

My bullying only revealed the paradox of attraction. That which attracted me repulsed me. I actually envied Richard's brilliance. The way he reticently laughed in response to the jokes I created to hurt him, snatching the power from my lips, was a brilliance I wanted to master. He seemed to be comfortable with and at home in his body. I wasn't good with my own.

Jamal, on the other hand, embodied all I had come to picture as my ultimate crush. His wavy hair was always sculpted into a precise fade that seemed to melt onto his smooth, handsome face. He was a corny mama's boy whom I let win when we mock-wrestled in the World Wrestling Federation ring we had built on our block when we were in middle school. He grew into one of the coolest and cutest boys in the neighborhood, donning the newest gear in the 1990s, like Filas and leather 8-Ball jackets. I was attracted to him—so much so I was willing to fight him to kill my attraction. We eventually fought in the middle of the street in front of everyone in our neighborhood. Someone else hit me in the head with brass knuckles as I punched the boy I hurt with words because I was too scared to let him know I really desired his friendship. Cruelty was a capacity I possessed as much as OB did.

The real tragedy of living with routine acts of violence is the way each act deadens emotions. Unfeeling was too common among many of us. We had felt too much about those we'd lost or feared losing, until death became something many of us began racing toward or away from. Many times, I felt that I was a nobody who felt nothing. As scholar Marc Lamont Hill argues in his book *Nobody: Casualties of America's War on the Vulnerable, from Ferguson to Flint and Beyond*, people "marked as poor, black, brown, immigrant, queer, or trans" are cast as nobodies caught up in web of interconnected oppression. But zeros are not nothings. They are something. And they are real. They exist, and they matter.

That day, I faced a probable ending. There could have been a fire, but there was no sacrifice to burn that day. And as a consequence, there were no ashes to be collected, no traces of a life to be discarded.

Somehow I managed to keep going after that incident. When I left my house with my head hung low, I would overhear Mark and his friends as they acted out what had happened. Mark would convulse, scream, and pretend to cry. The crowd would laugh and I would walk away, but with my head held a little higher than before. I had no choice but to go forward. There was no choice but to keep dreaming that the nightmare was over.

SHORTLY AFTER I WAS transferred to AT in the middle of eighth grade, and around the same time OB and his friends jumped me, I decided to apply to private schools. We did not have Google in 1990, so if we needed to find a phone number we had to search through the massive Yellow Pages. I searched for as many schools with the word "Friends" in the name as possible. Friends' schools had to be the best if Ms. Leary talked about them.

Ms. Leary, my former Language Arts teacher whose class I was in before I was transferred to AT, had taken on the responsibility of helping interested students apply to private schools on scholarship. I hated Ms. Leary, and I was certain she despised me. She was the other white teacher I had before Ms. Compo.

Ms. Compo encouraged us to work hard, but she did so without talking down to us as if her being was more than the sum total of the black students she taught. Ms. Leary didn't wear make-up, her hair was not coiffed and blonde, and her attire was not manicured like that of Ms. Compo. Her words were less careful, brasher, and sometimes hurtful in ways Ms. Compo's words were not. She once, for instance, said aloud in front of my classmates, "You can't write!" That was her response to an assignment I turned in. Looking back from my vantage point today, she was just a more honest white person—the type who said what she really thought rather than hiding the truth behind a smile. She was wrong for ridiculing me in front of my peers, but it's possible she saw my potential. Either way, I refused to ask her for help.

I was already wary of white teachers. Unlike the trust I had for Ms. Harrison, my black sixth-grade teacher who used every subject hour as an opportunity to teach us black history, or Mrs. Dunham, the black music teacher who took me home some weekends so I could sing as she played the piano, I did not trust white teachers enough to think they would support me. So I combed through the yellow pages in search of a school close in name to Moorestown Friends School, the school Ms. Leary raved about. The first one I found was Mullica Hill Friends School.

"Hi, my name is Diane Moore. My son is interested in your school and would like to apply."

My voice at fourteen was still shrill. Over the phone, I played the role of a concerned and loving thirty-year-old mother. Fueled by determination and my dreams, I contrived a story and, to my surprise, it worked. A few days later, an application package appeared in our mailbox.

Pictures of a field that was as lush as the grass on episodes of the *Little House on the Prairie* TV show, positioned opposite a few old brick buildings, caught my attention. The campus looked more modest than I had imagined, but I knew white families with money sent their kids to the school whether they were capable of achievement or not. The anticipation I felt as I read over the application was matched only by the joy I knew I would experience when I got to tell Ms. Leary I had been accepted to a Friends school without her help.

I completed the application by myself, including the requisite parent's essay. Ms. Leary insisted I couldn't write, but I guess she was wrong. I can't recall what I wrote, exactly, but I was invited to interview. I just needed to figure out a way to get there. I called the New Jersey Transit customer service hotline, gave a representative the address to the school, and asked for the best route. The trip would be an hour and a half. I traveled alone.

Walking from the bus stop to the campus, I noticed that the houses seemed to expand the closer I got. The roads stretched wider and contained fewer cars. At the center of Mullica Hill were antique stores and eateries I had only seen on television. The pace was slower. And the kids, mostly white and seemingly happy, were not Ms. Leary or Ms. Compo white. They seemed like the type of white people who stayed far away from the streets I traveled to get there.

The head of the school interviewed me. Teacher John, as he was called, was an older and friendly white man whose balding silver hair capped his head. He took me on a tour of the school. I wasn't overwhelmed when chatting with teachers whom the students called by their first names. They liked me enough to accept me. I would soon begin grade nine in a school that cost several thousand dollars to attend. I told my mom without a clue as to where the money would come from.

"I'm going to Mullica Hill Friends School," I said without flinching.

"You going where?" Mom had no clue I had applied and even less of a clue about how she would pay.

My mom and I didn't talk about my actions. If she was worried about the potential financial burden or my safety, I didn't know it at the time. When I asked her later what she really thought, she was candid. "It's good when you can look back and laugh at good times, but back then I was thinking: *Where does this boy think I work?* I was happy at the same time because it showed how smart you were. After all, I was a teenage mom and having to hear my children and I were going to be nothing, I felt like, *Wow.*"

She knew she could not afford tuition with the $300 she made each paycheck moving heavy boxes at Bradlee's. In the fall of 1990, the federal minimum wage was $3.80. The median income of black families led by a single woman in 1990 was $12,130, a tiny increase from $11,080, the median income for the same group in 1967. The median income of white families at the time was three times that number. My mom's approximate pretax annual wages of $7,904 placed her far below the median income of black families led by single woman. We were quantitatively poor, but I was not deterred.

I ended up attending the school, to the astonishment of my family. Friends School provided me with a financial aid package, and my grandfather George agreed to help cover the balance. It was a selfish act on my part. Chasing my dream meant my mother, grandparents, and aunts would have to reel in their own for my benefit. The money for bus fare, lunches, school trips, school supplies, and clothes was a sacrifice my family took on without having been asked—in ways so many of the black families in my neighborhood did for their own.

When school started in the fall of 1990, my days began at 4:30 a.m., when Mom would wake me up while the sky was still midnight blue. My father was in prison at the time. My younger sisters would sleep in and prepare for school a few hours after I left. I waited at the bus stop with black working-poor adults in Camden who braved cold, heat, and exhaustion to get to work every day. There I would take the 400 bus from my neighborhood to the transportation center downtown and then the 411 bus from downtown to the suburb of Woodbury, where my aunt Ruth lived, and there a small yellow school bus would pick me up to take me to the school I had lied my way into.

All of this transpired around the same time OB and his friends doused me with gasoline. Little did they know their act of aggression would motivate me to chase my dreams and claim the future they tried to snuff. People who are always under siege often have no choice but to conjure their inner powers, to manipulate energies as they walk down streets where they were once beaten, to bend sound waves when invectives are close enough to the ear to cause pain, to suture broken hearts when the people they love refuse to love them back, and to appear again and again after death attempts to disappear them.

Convulsing, crying, screaming, or not, I was set to win. My survival depended on my ability to fight back. Later I would learn to use my fists, but this time I relied on my agility and ran in the direction of freedom. At some point, even the most fearless and cunning among us won't be able to contort our bodies to escape a homo-hating person's bullet or summon the courage to refuse a bottle of pills calling out to be swallowed. But throughout my life, especially during my childhood, I did all I could to survive. I had no choice.

"I OUGHTTA SHOOT THIS motherfucker!" I was traveling home on the A train headed into Brooklyn in 2013 when another passenger uttered those words.

He had been ranting about "faggots" and noticed me as I stood by the subway doors not too far from where he was seated. I wasn't sure what gave the mysterious black man the impression I was a "faggot." I was wearing a bowtie and formfitting jeans. I tend to move my hands without restraint, which may have given him the impression I was gay. So often people's outward expressions are interpreted as signs for their sexual desires. And so often the gaze of the voyeur is inexact.

Even if the interpretation is correct, the reactions are mostly always wrong.

The subway car was packed, as it was most days during rush hour. The train was running express and jolted past the local stops. Each stop the train skirted was a horrifying reminder that it would be several additional minutes before the door I leaned on opened again. I wanted out.

The man continued to mumble the ways he would kill homosexuals if he had his gun. He said all of that while looking in my direction. Not one person intervened. All of the passengers heard him, but there was silence. Like me, they probably believed him. Throughout my life, I had witnessed what aversions to difference can bring about. A black boy's body soaked with gasoline as if it was prepared for sacrifice, a black boy's jaw so sore and swollen because it had been hammered by two older black boys' fists, a black boy's eyes fixed on the water under the bridge he was nearly thrown over, and a black boy's spirit invigorating itself after the body it dwells in was broken. I was that black boy and those are my memories.

I eventually exited the train with my life and bowtie intact, but I was transported back to moments during my childhood when similar acts of violence occurred in public, among silent witnesses. It reignited feelings of anxiety, fear, and hopelessness. I was hurt by others and nearly killed as a teen, but I refused to move through life as a victim. And on that train, standing squarely in front of a stranger threatening to shoot me, I owned my power yet again. But that work, the act of living in spite of harm, is not the sole responsibility of the persons always positioned on the receiving end of violence.

With all of the information the public has access to regarding the lives of black LGBT and gender nonconforming people, the heart of our society is hardened still. LGBT youth are subjected to harsh treatment in their homes, schools, and spiritual communities. They traverse streets that sometimes double as sites of murder. The reality that LGBT youth are disproportionately affected by homelessness, over-policing in their neighborhoods, and biased treatment within health care institutions is well documented. Trans women of color are murdered at alarming rates, yet these appalling crimes are recast in media headlines without widespread heartbreak or a call to action. The myth of black gay economic progress is tempered by the reality that many black LGBT people carry the weight of poverty. Some do not survive the journey. Attempts to love, marry, have sex, and use public restrooms without the interference of states, municipalities, and businesses are undertakings that require courage and trust. But it is hard to put faith in systems that render you a throwaway. Black LGBT people are not the amoral problems deserving of what has been inflicted upon us, nor are we victims who refuse to fight back or sometimes die while trying. The more precise rendering of the problem is one that exposes both victimizers and an apathetic public that allows bias, violence, and hatred to continue under its watch.

Too many of the strong have died at the hands of the weak, and the silence of those who supposedly love us has been the loudest response. Those of us alive to tell our stories do so because our testimonies counteract the silence and are a demand for safety, love, and life. And whether we are mocked or killed while giving voice, the lasting sound of our individual and collective voices remain as evidence of matchless endurance.

Chapter 4

TOUCH

Our small living room in Crestfair was barely lit by the glow of the TV. The room was quiet as our intense breaths became a backdrop for play. Our naked bodies, mine slimmer than his, not yet pubescent, touched as we drifted between fantasy and reality. Electricity raced down my arm until it landed at the tip of my finger when I touched him. As he kissed my lips. As he looked over areas of my body I had yet to love. I sensed we had crossed a line.

Kissing Terrence felt different than those moments when I experimented with my girl cousins. I experimented with cousins, as some children do, and learned what it takes to awaken urges in our bodies. We were all too young to kiss, to be naked, to have play sex. But something was unusual that night with Terrence. I wasn't coerced as I had been in the past, and Terrence was a boy. He was my best friend and the first boy I kissed. I was nine. We lived in the same apartment complex and both of us attended H. B. Wilson Elementary School. He stayed over at my house on a few occasions. And during one of his visits he asked me to do with him what the characters—white and adult—were doing to each other in a soft-porn episode on HBO.

Fully developed white bodies, wet with sweat, moved across the screen on the floor-model television behind us. We muted the sound and watched the movie. We watched their lips touch as the man's hand gripped the woman's breasts. My heart was beating fast as the blood rushed through my body, but I was scared my mom would wake up and catch us. Touching Terrence would only be possible if she continued to sleep. She did.

I sensed then I had broken a rule that I would later learn is unbreakable, but I wanted more lines to cross. Feeling a body was new; feeling a boy's body was new; feeling this excitement in my body was new. It wouldn't remain new for long. I would break that silently understood rule again and again in search of the electricity that consumed me as we played in the dark with the TV on mute and my friend's lips touching mine.

Like so many black boys who would grow up to love and lust after other boys, I would have died had I not found safety in my imagination. I maneuvered through my days, smiling even as I suffocated in a world that refused to let me breathe. Early on, I learned how to protect and nurture my desire for same-sex intimacy, long before I began searching for touch in eerie parks and strangers' beds. I was terrified and stimulated by the sparks that charged my body when I was in the presence of certain black boys. My boyhood crushes would never know, but I conjured impossible romance dreams in which black boy affection was ordinary.

I landed over and over in the arms of the type of black boys who protected me in dreams but harmed me in real life— the boys I would later end up hurting, too. I was attracted to what I could not have and to what I wanted to be: straight, masculine, athletic, and attractive. This particular boy was the model, the acceptable boy on his way to becoming the black man other boys would emulate. So I dreamt him into existence, and he became the type of black boy I wanted to love. And in my fantasies I imagined the kind of attraction I knew could exist but was concealed in public. I only wanted what other black kids seemed to experience during their teen years.

Other kids, like my sisters and cousins, would run home out of breath just to make sure that anticipated phone call from a crush wasn't missed. And after the call—while their eyes still sparkled and butterflies flitted in their stomachs—mom, dad, older cousin, little sister, aunt, or friend would ask about the youthful love, remembering for themselves how each minute away from a crush turns into long, agonizing hours.

Who is she?

How does he look?

You mean the light-skinned one?

Y'all boyfriend and girlfriend?

Some kids, with a gaze of ecstatic optimism on blushed faces, responded to the queries with truth. But I never had answers, and when I did I lied, because I was always asked the wrong questions, if I was asked any questions at all.

Elementary school and middle school teachers who taught mostly black kids in the schools I attended talked only about white love and heterosexual desire. Nothing I was taught or read seemed connected to Terrence's kiss. I read *Romeo and*

Juliet during my time in Ms. Compo's AT Language Arts class in eighth grade. And we responded to the expected questions: *How did you react when Romeo and Juliet kissed without even knowing each other's names? Why do you think they decided to die together rather than live apart? That's some powerful love.* That same year, I wanted my neighbor Cynthia to be my girlfriend. That same year, I was too nervous to be around her older brother because I feared and wanted him. His body was sculpted like a wrestler's and his swag wasn't too pronounced. He was cool, but not too cool to hang out with me. That same year, I started watching my Uncle Mike's straight porn when he and my Aunt Ella would leave for work. The year after Philadelphia-based black gay activist and writer Joseph Beam's second anthology was posthumously published by his mother, Dorothy Beam, and his friend, Essex Hemphill.

In 1986, when I was ten years old, Joseph Beam edited the first anthology of writings by black gay men in the United States. It was the same year the International Committee on the Taxonomy of Viruses officially named the human immunodeficiency virus (HIV) as the virus that causes AIDS. The World Health Organization (WHO) had reported tens of thousands of people were living with AIDS in 1986. In October of that year, US surgeon general C. Everett Koop issued the *Surgeon General's Report on Acquired Immune Deficiency Syndrome*, which urged educators and parents to begin talking to children, as early as elementary school, about AIDS and condom use. The 1986 report failed to encourage adult caregivers to talk with young people about same-sex desire and sex. I had kissed Terrence just one year before. No one talked to me.

The government's overwhelming focus was on protecting the bodies they deemed as vulnerable from those they saw as cursed and lewd deviants. Rep. William Dannemeyer from Orange County, California, read a statement into the *Congressional Record* on June 29, 1989. It is an example of the type of prejudiced talk that shaped the public's understanding of queer and trans people. During his speech, entitled "What Homosexuals Do," Rep. Dannemeyer famously described the sexual acts gay men purportedly partake in like "rimming, or one man using his tongue to lick the rectum of another man; golden showers, having one man or men urinate on another man or men; fisting or handballing, which has one man insert his hand and/or part of his arm into another man's rectum; and using what are euphemistically termed 'toys' such as one man inserting dildoes, certain vegetables, or light bulbs up another man's rectum."

I was thirteen years old when Rep. Dannemeyer described the distinctive magnetism I experienced when I looked into the eyes of another boy as if it were sodomy. The twin forces of shame and stigma penetrated the lives and psyches of black queer and trans people. The state's refusal to name same-sex desire as acceptable and separate from the AIDS epidemic was piercing. Queer desire wasn't normal. If it were, I would not have been forced to hide my attraction to boys for the sake of others' comfort. I would not have felt I should lie repeatedly about having a girlfriend or about having sex with said fictional girlfriend or force myself to date a girl just so I could tell the truth when someone asked. The social cues pointed out to me my budding strangeness. But "normal" is a pass afforded only to those who are too scared to dream, too afraid to transgress. Queerness is a way of life people fear because in it they might find freedom. But I was caged for a long time before I took hold of my liberation.

In 1990, when Ms. Compo invited my peers and me into the fictional world of the white couple from Verona, she spoke with elegance about the complex beauty of love in the Middle Ages. Juliet and Romeo's world was not mine. I was a black gay boy from a working-poor family growing up in the age of AIDS, in an impoverished black American city, within a society antagonistic to LGBT people, in a country that had yet to value black love and bodies. Certainly, black queer love would be dismissed as an impossibility.

Teachers and adult family members never spoke Joseph Beam's name to me. No one was brave enough to search out his story. No one told me that a short ten-minute car ride from Camden black gay men like Beam were living and fighting for the black queer futures I dreamt of in isolation. No one placed *In the Life* or *Brother to Brother* on course syllabi or in my backpack. I read that story about white heterosexual young love while black boys and men across the United States died tragic AIDS-related deaths because they sought affirmation, familiarity, love, and sex from one another.

I was unaware of Beam's work or of our histories until I searched them out as an adult. The lives of the black men before me were compilations of tragic love stories and shatter-proof intimacy, invisibility and dogged strength, but estrange-ment was a common theme. The black queer body divorced from its desire. The black queer person treated as less than human. The forced silences black men were subjected to in their homes and broader communities. The consequences of black queer desire seemed more lethal than poetic. And I did everything in my power to resist becoming what I sensed so-ciety hated. I did not want to be so visible and, yet, unseen. I would think about Keith, my aunt Arlene's close friend, whom I assumed was gay. Keith was a hairstylist whose wrists moved too freely, whose words twirled from his lips, and whose walk was more of a cascading saunter than a hustle. He seemed to possess the inventiveness and buoyancy I lacked, and others hated him for it. I always wanted to know who it was he loved and desired, and whether our longings were the same. But I didn't ask.

Not one of my teachers ever revealed that queerness was the magic expressing itself in and through my black body, shaping my wishes, and pushing me toward the night. But much later in my life, when I returned to the story I read as a teen, I realized when Romeo spoke of love as "a smoke raised with the fume of sighs / Being purged, a fire sparkling in lov-ers' eyes / Being vexed a sea nourish'd with loving tears," was he not talking about the vaporous desire clouding my dreams?

I too experienced the type of love Shakespeare called "a preserving sweet." Joseph Beam named this love, the act of a black man loving a black man, "revolutionary."

JASON WAS FIFTEEN, a year younger than me, when we met. My mother, sisters and I lived with my grandparents at the time. His buff-brown face had an occasional pimple. The tiny hairs on his chin touched my hand like the thin, needled edges of a brush. Five feet, six inches tall and built like a football player, he walked with an air of meticulous cool, fully present in his body and fully aware that he was the shit. He was a ladies' man. He dated Vicki, one of my closest female friends. And nearly every night for a year, Jason would sleep over at my house. It made it easier for him to see Vicki because she lived across the street. But no one knew he and I would sleep in the same twin-sized bed placed in the cement-walled bedroom in the back of our messy and dark basement. Even when the basement flooded, smelling of sewage, he was there slowly moving his body closer to mine—inch by inch, minute by minute.

Every night, he would call his mom. She would give him permission to sleep over. We would hang out on the porch. I would observe as he and Vicki flirted or argued. And every night, we would end up at my house, in the basement, and in the bed I moved to from the couch I previously slept on after my uncle moved out. I would lie closest to the wall. I would act as if Vicki no longer existed. I knew it was wrong, but it felt right. We slept in boxers and T-shirts. I would watch him take off his clothes, baring chiseled brown arms and legs. Boxers loose, exposing a body more mature than my own. He would lie down in the bed. Silent.

For hours, we listened to the breath flowing in and out of our mouths. And like clockwork, after an hour of adjusting our bodies, Jason would end up in my arms. Close. Close enough that he could feel my body react to the feel of his skin and the quiet expression of unspoken attraction. Close. So close, the sweat from our bodies would moisten our underclothes. Close enough to cause me to forget my dad's absence, my family's financial constraints, or the potential conflicts that awaited me when I left the house for school the next day. It wasn't sex. We were just close. So close I could sense his fears emanating from his body without him ever whispering a word. What we shared was touch and intimacy.

We cared for each other. He wouldn't tell me he loved me, but I knew he did. Why else would he stay in my basement nearly every night, only to fall asleep to the sound of mice playing in the dark as they moved through pipes and across the cold cement floor?

We were connected. And, yet, our mouths never spoke the words that our bodies and spirits called for every night. Only once did he ask me with humor and juvenile boldness, "Can you suck my dick?" I giggled because I was too stunned to say anything in response. He playfully grabbed my head, moving it in the direction of his crotch. "Nah! You crazy as hell." I continued to play along as if I didn't know his joke wasn't a joke at all. I wanted to do it, but what we shared was enough. No one knew. No one asked me about Jason.

I never expressed the full range of emotions I felt. For many black boys and girls who are attracted to the same sex, black queer life is a life of solitary confinement. Love didn't feel quite like love because I couldn't speak it out loud. Unlike some black teens who had friends, family members, and other adults to share secrets with or to ask questions, I had no one. The type of love I wanted to experience didn't seem to exist for others. And not having counsel, examples, or the safety and freedom to express my longings at home and at school meant that I spent many days desiring freedom from captivity. I imagined the questions I wanted family members to ask. I also imagined my responses. *Who is that cute boy you were with? You seem to brighten up whenever he is around. What do you love about him? Does he make you smile? Does he make you laugh? Do you feel safe?* "Yes. Yes. Yes," I would respond. Freedom.

People who have been caged too long will do anything to get free. By the end of my high school years, I ran into the dark. Secretly talking to men on phone chat lines. Messing around with classmates I would introduce as "friends." I assumed my family didn't know I had sex when they left for work or school. I wasn't certain they cared. This was the world that shame and stigma created, a world full of loud silences.

I SWALLOWED AND DIGESTED my secret. The aftertaste of my week with him was so unforgettable I would stick a finger down my throat to bring it up years later. Billy was his name. He was in his early twenties and stood a few inches taller than me. His agile body was buried under an army fatigue coat and baggy jeans. Hypnotic eyes lit Billy's smooth honey-colored face and tempting smile. His measured movements through the thorny paths of the public park in Center City Philly made him seem unafraid.

We briefly played the game. I turned around and looked in his direction as he walked away. We caught eyes as he glanced back. He nodded. My heart raced as we gave each other the look that is understood only by two young men searching for each other in the night. Our gaze was our contract.

There were no words spoken. No unease. Just unfulfilled longings and erotic attraction doing for us what our silences in the day had prevented. Dead brown leaves crunching under our feet was the only sound we made as we searched in the dark for a place to go. I was too scared to actually fuck a stranger outside. Trees aren't mattresses. Police patrolling parks aren't friends. And homosexuality wasn't right. But because welcoming embraces were few, the hand of a stranger moving about my neck as I unzipped my pants was worth it.

We didn't do much, but our too little was enough. Jerking off with an unexpected stranger outside amid quieted moans competing with the sounds of cars traveling in the distance, close enough to hear the breath of other men cruising the park, was a new experience for me. I was nineteen. I wasn't yet gay.

Billy was just my third or fourth secret. Always in the dark of the night and always alone, I found touch and, sometimes, violence. Not that time, however. I searched and left the park with an answered prayer. It was a peculiar blessing, not unlike Terrence's innocent kiss or Jason's hugs that fueled my wet dreams every night. Those encounters were so memorable because they represented the fantastic, surreal power of fugitive freedom. Queerness is magic for those brave enough to make use of it, but it can feel poisonous for those who have yet to give in to its power. I sensed Billy's magic.

So I traveled with Billy to his home in northwest Philly. No overnight bag or change of clothes. No toothbrush or condoms. No clue how I would get home and no contact with friends for several days. No cares in the world, including for myself. No money. No sense of Billy's last name. But we held each other every night.

For that short time when we lost ourselves in our sweat, stale breath, and questions, there was no abandonment or fear of rejection. In Billy's cluttered ten-by-twelve-foot room, our bodies intertwined. We shared secrets we would later forget. We giggled at horrible jokes. In his wisdom, Billy encouraged me to push through college. We held hands. Listened to music. Only the faint concerns of acquiring HIV after days of unprotected sex broke our harmony, but even the thought was not enough of a warning to convince me to leave or get condoms. How could I? The presence of arms and hands and tender lips and empathic hugs and loving thrusts and seeing eyes was too irresistible for me to fear death.

I had buried my fear of HIV years before when my aunt Cookie told me, at the age of fifteen, that a second cousin I had never met was gay. She didn't actually say the word. She made a hand motion others used when they wanted to communicate that someone they knew was a fag. And for the fag, wrists, like any dream of his desires for acceptable intimacy, seemed to always be broken. Aunt Cookie quickly added, "Your cousin's name was Darnell, too. He died of AIDS." Her semantics game worked. I would never again say "AIDS" and "gay" without interpreting them as synonyms. My fate was sealed. I was gay and, therefore, AIDS would be my fate, just like my dead, gay, HIV-positive cousin whom I had never met, who may have existed only in Aunt Cookie's imagination.

But I kept my cousin alive in my dreams. I imagined that his skin was smooth and as brown as maple. His eyes were deep and dark. His hands were strong, but smooth enough to be held by the hands of another man. His back was perfectly postured, strong enough to carry his lover from the sofa to the bedroom. He was the black man I learned to openly shame and secretly admire. He was my aunt's friend Keith. He was LeRoy, my high school classmate who jumped double-dutch better than the girls. He was Dre, who told me I was gay before I knew I was, who was hurt because I messed around with his boyfriend like I messed around with our mutual friend

Ramik's crush. Dre died before I knew what was wrong; he was buried along with his secrets. This was the imaginative world black men like us, who flirted with, fucked, and deeply loved other black boys and men, tried our best to survive—despite the ways HIV decimated those around us in the 1990s.

Some of these men—sometimes beloved and sometimes scorned—were our fathers, uncles, neighbors, boyfriends, hookups, and play mothers. So many of us were and are living through the post-traumatic anxieties of those years. Public health research and community-based interventions then and now focus on the "who" and not the "why" when it comes to advocacy related to black boys and men and HIV. During my late adolescence, never once did a doctor ask me, while administering an HIV test, if I experienced love or rejection, connection or estrangement. It didn't matter that Billy was beautiful and kind. They wanted to know if I had sex with men. They didn't ask why it was I decided against using a condom despite my awareness of HIV risks. It didn't matter that I never had sex with Jason, who didn't identify as "gay" or "bi" then or now, and yet shared care and intimacy with him. Some doctors didn't even smile while interrogating me. Some never asked if I was okay, because my feelings were not their concern. Humans feel, but subjects report.

Black boys and men are read as hypersexual: strong enough to deal with anything that comes our way, possessed of a brutish masculinity that prevents us from feeling, enabling us to terrorize others' bodies. Our dicks are caricatured as weapons or photographed as objects of desire poking out from our clothes, the only part of our bodies that's coveted. Our eyes as lacking tears. Our hands as tools for violence or pleasure, but little in between. Our lives as worthy of quick conclusions.

Whether my fate as a black man in love with other men was God's retribution or some form of nature correcting the unnatural, Aunt Cookie's words haunted me like a divine foretelling. And as long as I would die from AIDS, fucking and being fucked raw by Billy in his strange row house in Philly would be of no consequence. I imagined death to be sweeter when the dying didn't die alone, so I sought other bodies as company. If loneliness and rejection are the worst deaths, I had died many times before.

Ramik eventually picked me up from Billy's house several days after I had disappeared. He was noticeably worried and upset. I was less so. Billy was the secret I had been hoping to find. Weeks before, I had walked the northern end of Thirteenth Street in Philly under the light of day. It was the corridor where queer and mostly black trans women sex workers strolled for jobs. That day, for about one hour, I walked the street, too, in search of a man who would show up in a car willing to look me in the eyes, to hold me as if I were deserving of love. I was in search of a man who, like my father, would stand before me bare and offer me safety. No one picked me up that day. My heart broke. This, too, is the stuff of black boys' dreams.

But then, somewhere in the dark of the night in that park in Philly, I lost myself because I had longed so badly to be found. Billy found me. It was strange love. We tend to hide the desires we've been taught to be ashamed of. And the things we are ashamed of we tend to desire the most. Like so many black boys and men, I did not show up in a park or have sex with a strange man for the reasons most people suspect.

Pleasure and survival, touch and attraction, are not so easily pulled apart. I met up with another man in a park, turned to his body, sought refuge in his arms and in his bedroom, fucked, and disappeared for days with him because I located unspoken desires where they could not be found elsewhere. Not in sex education classes, living rooms, church sanctuaries, workplaces, or state institutions. And I was willing to deal with the consequences because I believed, because I had been told, that I would be infected and deadened anyway.

These actions tend to be the consequence of a twisted self-fulfilling prophecy we are socialized to believe. Too few are asking us the questions to get to the depths of black queer boys' traumas. *What is it that you desire but have been denied? What is it that you need to feel safe? How do you actually feel about the person you had sex with? What is it about him you desire? What are the sources of your pain? Who hurt you? Who first told you that your sexual desires and attractions were wrong? Does it feel better when you use a condom? Do you feel more connected when you don't use a condom at all? What is about that particular connection that fulfills you?*

To ask those questions would mean black boys and men would have to be seen, first, as bleeding, crying, vulnerable, and sometimes resilient human persons. We are breakable. Black boys and men are still going to parks. They are searching for an embrace and sex with another man or woman, the butterflies that dance in the stomach when a crush says hello, relief from estrangement, pleasure, comfort, and so much else people across the spectrum of sexualities are in search of. Black same-sex love is revolutionary because we must first convince ourselves we are deserving of receiving and giving what has been denied us for so long.

Joseph Beam wrote about black same-sex love as a revolutionary act in the 1980s. He died at the young age of thirty-four without fully experiencing the love he theorized. A few years ago, when I was a couple of years older than Beam was at the time of his death, I read a draft of an essay written by Beam's close friend Colin Robinson, a black gay writer and activist.

Robinson's essay was chilling. Love, he noted, was the focus of much of Beam's attention in his works. But Robinson lamented Beam's struggle to receive love. I was petrified. I tossed the pages across my room. I didn't want to live like that. *Please don't let me die like him. I don't want to write about a thing I cannot experience.* I resented Beam because I realized we were the same: dreamers moving through a world not yet prepared for the manifestation of radical visions of black queer love. Love is not available to those of us deemed disposable and unlovable. But we make love real, attainable, and felt anyway.

The human spirit breaks when longings so human, so acceptable to everyone else are denied. Homophobia is the strong hand that strangles the desires of those too vulnerable to undo its firm grasp. Lovelessness is a consequence of living in a queer-hating society. It shapes relationships between black men who love men, just as it shapes our relationship to the communities we exist in. We've been denied love. And some of us have sought out what we could to fill the gaping wells drained dry by a society that taught us to hate ourselves. But like cunning magicians, many of us have learned to break ourselves out of our cages even when those attempting to master our lives keep fervent hold of the keys.

Chapter 5

RUN

I stared out the window from the backseat of Dre's car, wishing I could escape the trap that he had set. The discomfort and embarrassment, the sweat forming under my armpits and wetting the T-shirt I wore under layers of baggy clothes, intensified as we made our way down the long stretch of suburban roads to Franklinville Skating Rink one winter night in '94.

I tried to figure out the best way to respond to the questions being posed by my three closest friends. I wanted to say something to convince them to understand that what they believed to be my truth was a lie.

"I know you are gay, so why don't you just admit it. You like boys!" Dre blurted out in his typical cutting manner as Tariq and Ramik giggled.

Dre was a free spirit. A year older than me, he had learned to move through the streets of Camden with little care about others' thoughts. He passed through crowds with grace, his hips rocking from side to side. Even when peers accused him of switching like a girl, he would walk upright with self-possession and strength. He talked with a slight lisp that shaped the end of sentences. And he moved willowy, without the rigid calculations made by most of the black boys I grew up around who tried their best not to be soft.

They had good reason. If some critics in media, academia, and the cloistered class of upwardly mobile black people were correct in the 1990s, black boys channeling relentless hardness on the streets of urban America was the consequence of gangsta rap. Popular hip-hop groups like N.W.A (Niggaz Wit Attitudes) were one of the explanations for the seeming downward spiral of a generation of black youth who cussed too much, sagged our pants too low, and behaved like thugs in the streets—as if to those critics hip-hop, and gangsta rap in particular, were not cultural inventions created in response to the various social conditions young black and Latino people faced. The so-called war on drugs and the dizzying impact of poverty within Camden had as much to do with young black people's need to be seen as unbreakable as our desire to be more gangsta than Eazy-E.

National events in the mid-1990s created an environment that encouraged the performance of bravado among black youth who lived in urban cities then. I was one of many black young people across the country who watched in horror as Rodney King, a black taxi driver, was brutally beaten by four white Los Angeles police officers after he was apprehended after a high-speed chase in 1991. The kicks to the face, the punches to his body, the blood pouring onto the streets were reminiscent of police practices common in places like Camden. After the four officers were acquitted in 1992, the city of LA went up in flames as black people, weary and outraged, once again, rebelled and burned shit down because of the state's quick move to justify its violent, racist practices against black people.

The release of KRS-One's fiery anthem "Black Cop" in 1993 was a song black teens recited as if the lyrics—"Stop shootin black people"—were Gospel. That same year a black cop singled me out while walking to my aunt's house after school because he assumed I was a "lookout boy." After he physically assaulted me, placed me in his car without reading me my rights, and left me to walk home a few miles from where he picked me up, I distrusted and hated police more than ever before. What the black cop did not know was the effect his actions would have on my heart and psyche. That is one of the reasons, besides the lure of male dominance, so many of the boys I grew up around worked so hard to not be soft. It hardened me.

A year later, America's "first black president," Bill Clinton, would sign into the law the Violent Crime Control and Law Enforcement Act of 1994, which placed 100,000 new police officers on the street and shepherded billions of dollars into the jail and prison systems. By then, they had already been bloated by an increasing influx of people—especially those who were poor, black, Latino, and indigenous—many of whom were caged for offenses like traffic stops, drug possession, and loitering. At the end of 1994, 1,053,738 people were incarcerated in federal and state correctional facilities, according to the Bureau of Justice Statistics. But by the end of June 1995, nine months after the crime bill was signed into law, the Department of Justice recorded the largest one-year increase in its history, accounting for the 1,104,074 people caged within its institutions. Closer to home, the ripple effects of the wars waged against drugs and crime resembled an epic gangsta movie.

In the late 1990s, the crack epidemic in Camden was in full swing. It had been built up by the underground work of an intricate network of traffickers, street-level trap boys and girls, and money-laundering state employees and officials. The streets were hot then. We referred to some sections of neighborhoods in Camden by the names of the drug sets in operation within them. After my day was over at Camden High, I would walk down Louis Avenue in Whitman Park, along a series of busy street corners known as the Hilltop. It was common when walking through Hilltop to accidentally step on tiny plastic baggies and glass vials emptied of the crack and weed they once contained. Quick-moving drug dealers, desperate users, and gang-like police units hovered around the corners, where fights, drug sales, and shootouts sometimes took place. Those were the effects of the crack epidemic I saw with my eyes, I was less aware of the causes.

A federal investigation would later reveal that some law enforcement officers, and even Mayor Milton Milan, received drug money in the 1990s. Milan, the city's first Latino mayor, was eventually found guilty of fourteen counts of corruption in December 2000. Strung-out men and women and street-savvy pushers were more obvious problems than the criminal masterminds in power behind the scenes like the mayor and police officers, profiting from the war they waged to supposedly end drug proliferation in our city.

Black youth in Camden did not have to rehearse and perfect the stories we heard in the rap songs we listened to. We did not orchestrate our dress and expressions to prove we were tough simply because we were poor young people growing up in an American hood. We only needed to look around at what was happening closest to us to see that our survival would come by our own hands, not at the behest of the state, which we thought aided most in our demise. And some of us, like Dre, were no less hard even as we learned to tap into the parts of ourselves that made us an easy target for both the state and some of our own people. I admired Dre, and I envied him. He had found a way to face the toughness of the world and still claim his freedom.

"What are you talking about? I am not gay. Stop trying to make me admit that shit just because you are."

I was in my senior year of high school, and I had yet to have sex with another boy. I had only had sexual encounters with girls and occasional moments of intimacy with Terrence and Jason. This was before Billy. So Dre had to be wrong. Yes, I was infatuated with Jason. It didn't matter that I could never forget Terrence's touch or that of another friend, Mikey, years after their imprints were left on my body. But I was also attracted to and flirted with Cynthia and "tomboy" Kim. I also promised Keisha, my girlfriend at seventeen, whom I was more attracted to as a friend than a sex partner, that we would marry. I was emotionally and sexually attracted to girls. I also dreamt about sex with boys.

The larger world made it clear that same-sex attraction was the type of evil that turns innocent boys into child molesters or freaks, and girls into man-hating dykes and aberrations. And a few of my gay friends seemed to believe maintaining a fluid attraction to whoever ignited my body at a given moment was akin to living as a fraud and sellout. My juvenile fascinations with sex and attraction were expansive, but the rest of society preferred desires to be either black or white, "gay" or "straight." I wouldn't know that I didn't need to confine myself until years later, after I had already compressed myself into an identity and way of life for the sake of the comfort of others, but never my own.

At seventeen, my secrets were still mine, locked away because of my faith in the sacredness of masculinity, which I assumed was a natural extension of heterosexuality. But there was a reason I befriended Dre, Ramik, and Tariq. I saw parts of myself in them, but I refused to admit that truth. I just regretted their ability to see parts of themselves in me.

"So, you mean to tell me you don't like boys? Whatever, girl!" Tariq chimed in.

"Yo, stop calling me a 'girl'! I ain't no damn 'girl,'" I hit back.

I wasn't as close to Tariq as I was to Ramik and Dre. Tariq was flashy, brash, and clockable. I stayed away from him because I did whatever I could to remain undetectable. Tariq's combination of clever wit and spiteful sarcasm was unmatched. I assumed he was quick to cut people down because he was tired of being called a "fat faggot." In my mind, and behind his back, that was also how I described him. He didn't match the image of the black gay boy I fantasized about then. He wasn't discreet. He wasn't manly. He didn't have an athletic build or sexy swag. I looked down on him for failing to live up to an ideal I too had failed to emulate. I despised him because he lived a life that wasn't a lie—in a big black body he loved.

Tariq bore his cross. But before long I sensed he had learned to protect himself from others' homophobic taunts and fat jokes by swinging insults instead of fists. He gave back what he received from peers like me. I knew for sure I would not entrust him with the details of my secret desires because I feared he would use my words against me.

Ramik and I had been friends since we were eleven. I lived in overlapping worlds that weren't as separate as I believed. Ramik helped me explore my inner life more deeply. He was one year younger and a grade level lower than me, but he was wiser and less afraid than I was. We watched each other grow up and asked questions and talked about sex, sexual identity, and boyhood without ever really recognizing that the thought-work we were doing would eventually save our lives.

I loved the plastic see-through boots he would wear during our high school years. My peers and I rocked crisp white K-Swiss and Reebok sneakers some of us would clean daily using a toothbrush and soap. When he decided to get hair extensions that were cut into a bob, I giggled out of affirmation and not embarrassment, even though I preferred the fly asymmetrical barber cuts that accentuated his debonair appearance. Every time he vowed to not give a fuck when people made jokes, I loved more and more the pieces of myself that others despised. Ramik allowed me to be. And that meant he never named me what I had yet to name myself. So I stayed under him like an eager student.

I stayed at Ramik's house often, and one time another friend of his was there. Ramik was protective of his relationships and made sure there was distance between those of us in his small orbit. I was surprised when he allowed his friend Sean and me to sleep over at the same time. Ramik fell asleep in his room and left his door slightly ajar. I wondered if he could sense the energy emerging not too far from where he laid his head. Did he know what would happen if he left us alone?

Sean and I were stretched out on blankets placed over the carpet on the living room floor. We whispered over the faint sound of the refrigerator. I can't remember exactly what we said. I do remember that my mind was overcome by panic and anticipation. It was hard to manage the defiant thoughts while my body invited pleasure.

"So, you ever mess with another dude before?" he asked.

"Nah! I haven't. I'm not gay," I responded. If by messing with a dude he meant fucking, I hadn't. But there were many boys I found attractive. He was one.

"You mean to tell me you wouldn't let another guy suck your dick if they paid you?" he asked, with a sly look on his face.

"How much money are you talking?" I smirked and giggled, but I knew what he was getting at. He wasn't intent on paying me, but I knew he was gauging my interest. My crafty response was my invitation, despite my trepidation.

Sean had seductive chestnut-brown eyes and a smooth, chiseled jawline like a model's. He was seventeen, but he was an experienced player. In the dark, on the floor, he moved closer. His hands were large and his touch was commanding. *No more words*, I thought. I lay there ready for him to prove to me that reality was better than my dreams, but I wasn't ready to deal with the ruins.

My heart was racing. I was so scared someone would walk in the room and see what we were doing, and turned on by the possibility of getting caught. His pinkish brown lips moved from my ear to my neck to my belly button. I could barely breathe. His head disappeared under the covers and between my legs. *No.* I wanted him to stop. I wanted to prove him wrong. *Yes.* I wanted him to keep going, so I moved my hand from my side to the top of his head. I wanted whatever I was feeling to never end. *No. Please stop.* The act, which felt so good, so right, suddenly felt so terrifying and wrong. Like a teacher, he promised me I would be okay, but I wasn't when it was over. Ejaculating while having sex with a boy was the ending of my life as I had come to know it.

I hastily put my clothes back on, pushed him away, curled up in a fetal position, and in the quiet of the night lay in utter horror until I was able to escape the anguish I experienced that early morning. I was a different person the next day. I no longer had any sense of what was to come. I was swept up by a dizzying array of emotions. My heart broke because I believed I had let so many people down—my family, my community, and others' God. And I cried, alone, in Ramik's bathroom. Sean, on the other hand, seemed fine.

There's a certain type of unrecognizable heartache that emerges when all one believes to be true comes crashing down like the illusory backdrop of a dramatic production. My innermost sensations, which I had denied in fear of others' judgment, felt fraudulent still. And I ended up disoriented as a result. The confusion I experienced wasn't unique. We expect young people to cross boundaries, break rules, and touch bodies for the first or second time, and most are supported as they work through their feelings. I lost sleep, however, because my dreams had become a nightmare I would face alone. I moved about like a zombie, dazed and lifeless, with no one to help process my disorientation or shame, and no one to giggle with when asked if I enjoyed my first *real* sexual experience with another boy on my best friend's living room floor. I no longer desired intimacy with another boy, at least in that moment. The tears and loneliness, faint breaths and confusion, palpitations and thrill, erections and desire, would have been less distracting had I found someone who could have offered their presence and support. I made a choice to have sex. I broke free from normalcy and was racked with paralyzing shame. But I wanted someone to affirm that I would still be good.

I walked into Ramik's room after Sean eventually left and stared at him, puzzled. I knew he could sense my pain as I whispered broken sentences with my head bowed low.

"What's wrong with you?"

"Uhm . . . I can't believe this . . . I feel like I'm gonna die. . . . Uhm . . . I messed around with Sean."

After my pitiful and dramatic confession, I looked up at Ramik's face and it went blank before he responded.

"See! This is why I keep my friends separate. That's why I don't let y'all stay over my house at the same time."

I understood why he was angry. We messed around in his house. He also confessed that he and Sean were dating. But all I could think about was the fact that I let another boy lick all over my body. Ramik went on and on, reprimanding me while I let my thoughts wander, trying to figure out what I could do to make the shame disappear.

I went home and tried to let the hot water from the shower cleanse my body until I could no longer smell or sense the residue of his tongue. The steam from the water filled the bathroom like a sauna. I prayed and asked God to forgive me and to help me forget the moans, our ecstasy, and the semen. When I finished I called Ramik on the phone and begged him for forgiveness.

Ramik was my go-to for answers. When he was mad at me, I called Dre. Dre was more than willing to listen and respond.

"I knew ya ass was gay. But why the hell did you choose Sean as the first person to fuck around with? Ramik is pissed," he said, with an air of disgusting satisfaction.

A night forever marked as my terrifying and terrific first sexual experience with another boy would now be remembered as the day I fucked around with my best friend's crush and nearly suffered a breakdown. I drifted on from that moment, and spent the remainder of my senior year in a haze.

College applications, SATs, and after-school employment were concerns second to my growing fascination with the life I imagined living beyond Camden's ten square miles, outside the caged sexuality that felt less comfortable after the taste of Sean's lips.

I spent the final months of my senior year roaming my imagination and the crowded hallways of Camden High School, the public school I transferred to after Mullica Hill Friends School closed its upper school division. I went from classrooms where I was one of two black students among no more than ten peers, mostly white and moneyed, to rooms overcrowded with black and Latino teens from working-poor families. By the time I arrived in 1992, a year past Camden High's centennial celebration, it was no longer considered the fabled public school where Camden youth went to manifest their dreams. The main building, made of gray stone, was called the Castle on the Hill. In Camden High's past, mostly

Jewish and Latino students walked through its doors, but in the 1990s, hundreds of black and Latino kids from all parts of the city entered the dwindling Castle each morning. When the composition of the student body changed, so did the tales of its splendor. The students I matriculated with, who were often cast as threats to the city's potential return to its glory days of white, middle-class ascension, sensed that we had been dealt a hand short of the kinds of cards necessary to win. But many of us were determined to prevail despite the lackluster resources provided.

By the time graduation neared, however, I was less concerned with achieving success as the American dream dictated: *Obtain a high school diploma. Go to college. Graduate. Leave home. And never return. Marry a woman. Have kids. Work. Pay off student loans. Buy a home. Buy a car. Repeat. Take vacations. Encourage my children to follow in my footsteps. Be declared successful.* Graduating from high school was a necessary goal, but only so I could be free. Free to explore the world outside the alley-like streets I knew as home. Free to recreate myself into a young man bestowed with the gift of magic and not the burden that comes with the curse of pretending. Free so I would no longer need to act my way through the awkward popularity contests high schoolers create to survive scrutiny by peers. Free so I would no longer shrink into a version of a self more hard and less expansive than the black boy I knew myself to be. No more energy wasted on discovering new routes from school to home to avoid crowds or harm. No more need for knives, brass knuckles, and makeshift weapons I carried to protect myself after too many robberies and fights—some of which I started. I knew if I was going to live life on my own terms, it would have to be away from what I knew and away from the cage of clichéd expectations, so I applied with little excitement and effort to the one college I would attend. Winning meant running. At least it seemed that way in the moment.

SETON HALL UNIVERSITY IS in South Orange, a short hour and a half drive from Camden, but it was far enough away from home for me to stumble into new experiences and fail outside the watchful gaze of those I feared shaming. It was also close enough to New York City. I had been to New York City only one other time in my life. I was sixteen when I traveled to the Statue of Liberty and the fabled Mamma Leone's restaurant, a once-popular eatery in Manhattan's Theater District. It was a trip organized by the summer youth entrepreneurship-training program Camden public schools offered in the 1990s. As I prepared to move onto campus, I held fast to my hopes of returning to the place big enough where the hyper-visible could be unseen, a place so worldly one could sin over and over again without the condemning stares that tend to be cast upon anyone who chooses to live as they will.. The skyscrapers and packed streets, the people who appeared to be raptured by wanderlust, those seeking to be discovered and those who walked about as if they did not want to be found, drew me in. I would one day roam those same streets, but until then the gated campus of Seton Hall would have to do.

We arrived in Newark, New Jersey, in the early afternoon of move-in day with bags full of my belongings. It was a humid early summer day in '94. The sounds of overworked commuters, train announcements, and incoming public buses filled the air. Aunt Barbara and I searched for signs leading us in the direction of the number 31 bus. We'd already been traveling for two hours, on the bus in Camden and on the train to Newark. Unlike others traveling to campus to begin a summer academic enrichment session meant to prepare students accepted through the Equal Opportunity Program (EOP), my family did not own a car. It was the second time I realized that our family lacked wealth. The first time, I was walking onto the campus of Mullica Hill Friends School, another microcosmic world where white middle-class and upwardly mobile black people sent their kids.

I was no stranger to long commutes, but the commute to Seton Hall made me more anxious than ever. I was moving away from Camden for the first time to a part of New Jersey I never imagined existed. Newark is a black city like Camden, but its spirit is animated, improvisational, and alive like jazz. The familiar tunes of Biggie Smalls and Craig Mack weren't as dominant as the house music blazing from the speakers on vendors' tables on Broad and Market Streets, where mix tapes with strange house beats like the "Percolator" and "Witch Doctor" were sold. Newark was a different world, a different hood, where people talked with a different tongue. The sound of the "r" was stronger, harder, as it rolled out of the mouths of the bold, hopeful, and aware black people from Brick City who seemed no less overcome by the looming presence of police and state neglect than those of us who grew up in Camden. Such is the illusion that shapes great escapes from home. The places I've run to seemed to always figure as mythical havens of possibility even if they were gripped by the same conditions that zapped hope out of the people and city I tried to abandon. Newark was no different. In fact, I would soon learn why black cities like Newark weren't that different in many ways from Camden.

My first year in undergrad was typical of that of any black eighteen-year-old from the hood dropped off and left alone with his bags and pipe dreams on the campus of a predominantly white university. And it wasn't just any predominantly white university; it was a Roman Catholic one, which meant I would need to prepare myself to face isolation and moral judgment for loving weed and men. White students, staff, faculty, and priests blanketed the campus from the dorms to the classrooms. Those of us who came through the EOP spent way too much time in the small EOP office because it was the one place where we knew other black and Latino students and staff would be. The university green sat at the heart of the campus, and during the welcome orientation it resembled an indie music festival where abundantly cheery white college students would meet up to eat medium-rare hamburgers and drink beers while the sun turned their skin red and scaly.

I registered for classes—a few I liked, a handful I skipped, and others I withdrew from. Even after graduating from a Camden middle school where I excelled as an "academically talented" student, struggling through two years of a private high school, being voted Camden High School's "Most Likely to Succeed" as a senior, and completing the EOP's summer program at Seton Hall, I was not prepared for a white campus. I hadn't learned how to navigate this strange world where white people's cares and well-being were centered.

No summer enrichment session I attended gave any indication that a white security guard would grab me and slam me to the ground. I was not taught to expect that a white baseball player throwing snowballs in front of our dorm during a late-night fire alarm would hit me in my face with a large piece of ice while he played. He had a black eye, and I was glad my fist would be remembered as the source. But it was no salve for the wounds to the soul resulting from racial profiling so normalized on a college campus. I felt as if justice, even at a Catholic university, was a concept that only made sense as a theory in philosophy and religion classes.

EOP counselors reminded us constantly to always sit in the front of the classroom, an effort to prepare us nonwhite students for academic success amid the prevailing presence of white peers and instructors. But cues and tips cannot replace the inner power you must summon, which gives you the courage to speak up (even when you don't have the energy) almost every time a white student or professor makes a racist claim they know to be truth. No words, no workshops, no constant reminders can distort your gaze such that you don't see that a majority of the students in the cafeteria are sitting and eating together, and they are all white. And the small pockets of black, Latino, and Asian students are cordoned off in small sections of tables. It might have been a scene from *Higher Learning*, John Singleton's cinematic take on racial division on predominantly white campuses, which came out in 1995, my second year at Seton Hall. Singleton's fictional account was too real and too right about a phenomenon so many nonwhite students at Seton Hall knew was unjust.

I had no living room full of black family members who would know I was hurting from loneliness just by looking in my eyes, no kin I could lean on who would remind me I belonged when I felt as if I did not deserve to be on the campus of a college I had put little effort into applying to. But their absences, amid the presence of the daunting reality of living black and free on a mostly white campus, forced me to shapeshift and fight.

By the end of my first year, I had helped reestablish the African Student Leadership Coalition with two first-year black girls, Tia and Kathy. We wanted our quest for respect and equity as black students at Seton Hall to extend beyond rants preached to the proverbial choir about the university's underrepresentation of black students, professors, and black student–centered groups and programs. I even ended up on Broad Street, the same street I walked on when I first traveled to Seton Hall with my Aunt Barbara, in Newark that year, but this time around I was one of a few dozen attendees packed in a discreet room in a barely finished building listening to black political prisoner and radical journalist Mumia Abu-Jamal. He shared his analyses of white supremacy, black politics, and incarceration by telephone. I was struck by his measured tone and enticing voice. Abu-Jamal was involuntarily isolated, restricting his ability to move past the door to his small prison cell in Pennsylvania. If Abu-Jamal's spirit could fly free in the midst of forced isolation, I was certain my black peers and I who willfully applied to Seton Hall could soar amid the restrictive whiteness of our university.

All of my life I had identified as black even if I sometimes, with or without awareness, distanced myself from black people I deemed too hood and poor even as others distanced themselves from me for the same reason. A world away from Camden, with little less than a year in the belly of a predominantly white campus, I had begun the process of a new becoming. I was becoming politically black: aware, awake, in love with my people, and enraged by racial injustice. I cared less about perfecting the appearances I had been taught to perform most of my life. I lost interest in those negotiations: displaying intelligence, knowing and staying in my place, quieting my voice, downplaying my street smarts so white people would not interpret me as a threat.

I changed—for better and worse. I walked around campus the first two years dressed in baggy gear and the hottest kicks I could purchase with the money left over from my many student loans or with credit cards I used without care. I cussed loudly, acted tough, and smoked blunts—all were tactics I employed to distance myself as far as possible from the white kids who walked past as if I were invisible and the black students who would remind me that niggas from Camden were worse off than all the rest. With pride, I would brag about Camden. Almost overnight, I had become the thing I was told to resist, a representation of the black thug from the hood. It was the one script I was most familiar with and the one I thought would protect me from white ignorance and set me apart from the black students whom I thought looked down on me for being less smart and not as refined as the rest. My act was deliberate, a survival tactic meant to protect me from the threat of erasure and homophobia. As long as my peers knew I could beat the hell out of white supremacy and white boys, and as long as they knew I could manipulate and fuck around with girls with more cunning sophistication than the other black boys, I knew I'd fare better than I had in high school. I was wrong. Even my avatars could not shield me from the inevitable onslaught of finger pointing and antagonism that accompanies difference.

FALL SEMESTER OF '95 I worked, as part of the student employment program, as one of several phone dispatchers whose job it was to call alumni of the university and solicit annual donations. The people I called rarely gave so I would sneak in calls to friends at home when I knew staff wasn't watching me. The alumni office was a few blocks away from the main campus. The money wasn't good, but it beat the few dollars I would receive for knocking on doors ensuring folks were registered to vote (for the particular candidates willing to pay us, of course) during election cycles. Work time was minimal, and after a few hours of acting as if my dignity was still intact while alumni screamed and demanded I never call their homes again, I would walk back to campus with Sinclair, a friend in my class from Camden. We vibed because we shared the same home, the same street smarts, the same swag, and the same point to prove: that we belonged. He came through the EOP summer program with me and was the other black boy fighting alongside me after the white boy athletes hit us with ice during their snowball fight.

One early evening after work, I asked Sinclair to wait for me while I used the restroom. I walked into the empty alumni office bathroom, unzipped my pants as I moved closer to the urinal, and briefly loss consciousness. It was a short ordeal. Short enough for me to grab hold of the urinal to keep from falling to the floor as I urinated. When I made it back outside Sinclair had a worried look on his face. "You alright? What's wrong? You don't look good, yo." I said very little in response. Something was wrong. Something was wrong with my body. Something I had never felt before.

I convinced him I was okay enough to walk the three long suburban blocks back to campus, where I could get a ride to the hospital. He ensured me he would get me to campus safely. What I didn't let him know was that I nearly landed on the bathroom floor. I didn't tell him I felt as if someone was scraping the inside of my chest with a blunt knife. Every step I took, the sharp pain intensified, and I staggered. Sinclair reached out his arms every few minutes to make sure I didn't fall over. We made it back to school, and I asked my friend Jewel to drive me to the hospital.

"What's wrong, Darnell? You are scaring me," Jewel asked with a worried look on her face.

I needed her presence at that moment because she seemed to possess a spiritual connection I lacked. She was a quirky black girl with a big laugh from the suburbs of central Jersey. We connected during the EOP summer program. We were close enough for me to know she had access to the God I once talked to as a child. I was scared and wasn't sure if I would live so I figured Jewel would know best how to communicate through prayer what I could not. I once asked God to rid our home of my father, even if that meant by death, and now I would need to ask to be saved from what I had wished upon my father.

I was losing strength. My chest felt like it had been punctured by an explosion of razors and I felt out of control. Jewel prayed, and I cried, as she drove feverishly to Orange Memorial Hospital, which was about ten minutes away from our campus and is now permanently closed. When we arrived at the emergency room, it was quiet and unsophisticated. Our university's student center seemed to be more active, and fitted with more technology, than the hospital's ER.

A white attendant checked me in. "Are you sure you don't want to get tested for an STD rather than have your heart checked?" she asked.

I was too weak to argue. But after she pulled Jewel to the side to inquire about our relationship, she informed me I needed to contact a parent or guardian right away. My EKG results were in. The nurse who had smirked thirty minutes earlier, leaving me to believe that my loss of consciousness had to do with a bout of gonorrhea or chlamydia, was no longer smiling. The nurses and doctor on call began moving around the ER quickly, talking in voices faint and serious enough to make me realize something was wrong.

"We need to talk to your mother right away, Darnell," the nurse demanded.

My eyes teared up. And Jewel started crying. "What's wrong? Please tell me what's wrong," I asked her.

But the nurse's response was the same: "We need to talk to your mother or a guardian right away."

I overheard the call. I couldn't make out all that was said, but I heard the words "myocardial infarction" and "helicopter." When the nurse returned, she broke the news.

"We are admitting you. You are in the middle of a heart attack. Your mother wanted us to have you transported closer to home but the only way that can happen is by sending you on a helicopter. Your mother is almost two hours away and you may not make it if you were sent down by ambulance."

I was nineteen. And broken. Bravado couldn't save me. The superhuman strength black boys' bodies are often imagined as possessing—resilient enough to take a punch or survive a bullet—wasn't there. I wanted my mama. And I wanted to live. I fell asleep after I was stabilized with medication, and when the nurse woke me up in the bed where I rested in the ICU the next morning, she softly uttered consoling words: "You had a rough night, young man."

While I slept, I had fought to survive. All I could remember was the dream that rocked my spirit until the tears I cried while begging God to let me live soaked my pillow enough for me to feel the damp residue in the early morning. My prayers were unlike the pleas to die I had uttered when I was younger. So many hours I spent contemplating death, longing to break away from the many hells I experienced on earth. I had come to believe very early on that my life would be cut short by sudden violence I encountered on the streets, by a scared police officer's gun, or by my own hands. I had never thought I'd fight so hard to live until death was near.

I was sharing a room with an older black man who was in his late sixties. His long body was attached to worn, calloused feet that seemed to have walked every inch of his life. He was a source of hope. One night he looked over and told me it made sense *he* was hospitalized while doctors prodded his body with needles, doing what they had to do to keep his heart functioning. But he assured me, "You are too damn young to be here. So whatever you've done to get yourself here, stop!" I took his encouragement to mean more than the need to stop smoking weed or commit to a healthier lifestyle. Up until then, I had done my best to welcome and speed death along. In my dreams and in my mind, I wanted out—until it was an actual option I needed to contend with.

I imagine the many black kids I grew up with—boys, girls, and those who eschewed those categories altogether—may have spent some time summoning an easy solution to the rampant violence we witnessed and the economic strains that choked our chances to thrive. The quick rush to death for me wasn't a morbid want for immortality; it was a quiet rebuke of the very real circumstances that hindered my survival. I didn't pick up a gun with the hopes of lodging a bullet in the chest of another kid. I didn't douse any of my neighbors with gasoline in order to kill them. I wasn't that father punching the mother of his children in the stomach or face. And I wasn't better than those who committed those actions. But I was black in a city wracked with poverty and political malfeasance, a person whose life was counted as a zero, who believed during certain moments that he didn't deserve to live.

Those who feel undesirable and worthy of death in a state that gives you no reason to believe you have a right to live tend to move quickly to accommodate those desires. But all I wanted when lying in the ICU, fighting a pain so indescribable, was to live. Living, as a black youth without access to the collective empathy and safety granted to white kids, is a weighty struggle.

The few diagnoses I received from the doctor varied from the possibility of coronary artery heart disease to drug-induced heart malfunction. My father suffered from an ongoing heart condition, and my youngest sister had heart surgery when she was a toddler. It was easy to believe I would face the same. I didn't want to tell my mom when she arrived a few days later, however, that I had smoked a lot of bad weed a few nights before. The weed was laced with PCP or cocaine, I assumed. I didn't want her to know I tried to test my awareness while high by working through basic multiplication problems I couldn't answer. So I remained silent about the potential cause of my condition that had me laid out in a hospital bed, known among residents as the youngest heart attack patient the hospital ever served.

Seven days later, I headed back to my family's home in Pennsauken, a small South Jersey suburban town bordering Camden. My mom and her husband, Lee, had moved into the three-bedroom home Lee's mom once lived in when I was a student at Camden High. My family turned the living room into my bedroom because I was instructed to limit my movement, especially up and down the stairs. A few days later, I underwent a heart catheterization at the Deborah Heart and Lung Center in Browns Mills, New Jersey, forty-five minutes from Pennsauken. The outpatient procedure lasted about an hour. My eyes widened as the doctor stood before me holding a long, thick needle containing a microscopic camera that would be inserted into an artery near my groin. The sight of the needle petrified me, but nothing was more startling than lying on a bed while nurses shaved my stomach and groin in front of my stepfather, who watched over the procedure with care. I will never forget the pain or the love.

I WAS OUT OF school during the spring semester of 1996. During my absence a friend admitted he had heard a rumor circulating on campus about my absence. "AIDS," he said. The rumor had apparently surfaced after my first boyfriend visited our campus.

Dae had traveled to Seton Hall a few months before I was placed on medical leave. Knowing he would drive his small, beat-up car more than an hour up the New Jersey Turnpike to check on me, fully aware I had yet to tell anyone on campus I had a partner, was the push I thought I needed to tap into my courage. I knew other students would inquire about the cute boy with a big grin, brown-sugar skin, wavy hair, and tight body walking with me across campus. I wanted them to wonder. As long as Dae's presence provoked questions, I knew I would have less explaining to do. If they were to spread rumors about me, they would at least have to acknowledge the dude I had been spending time with was fine as hell.

Dae and I met on Thanksgiving Day in '95. I first spotted him at the football game where Camden's competing high schools, Woodrow Wilson and Camden High, battled each year. He didn't know I noticed him as he moved through the crowd with grace and the confidence perfected by those convinced they owe strangers nothing more than their company. His presence was enough to attract me and cause me to push through hordes of people just to get another look at his face. He had smooth skin with tiny whiskers forming a mustache that matured his face, and dark brown eyes that lured me in. My instant connection to him was something I had not experienced before, one that caused me to whisper with sincere hope, "God, whoever he is, I want him to be my boyfriend."

Throughout my life, I had a knack for wishing for things others thought black boys were unlikely to obtain, like all As on my report cards and boyfriends. That evening one of my high school friends, Ricky, called to let me know he was in town. He invited me to go out with him and a friend to the Nile, a once popular gay club on Thirteenth Street in Philadelphia that black queer and trans people packed until the walls perspired. It has since closed, succumbing to gentrification in the popular part of town now known as the white "gayborhood." A year before, I would have said no. No one knew I messed around with guys except Ramik, Dre, and Tariq. But time spent at Seton Hall, far from home, opened up space for me to try new experiences away from the watchful eyes of those around me.

Ricky arrived at my house to pick me up. He wasn't alone. The passenger's silhouette was familiar; it was Dae.

"Wassup? I'm Dae."

He glanced back just enough to catch me staring at the side of his profile dumbfounded. I'm not sure if I even responded to his greeting. But as we drove, and he and Ricky talked just below the loud music blasting on the radio, I sat in the backseat thanking God. Someone, something, heard my prayer, because the boy who had quickened my heart earlier that day was now sitting close enough for me to smell and gaze at. That night in the club was unspectacular. The smells of bodies grooving to vogue beats and heavy liquor mixed. I danced a bit when the DJ played hip-hop beats, but I spent most of my time looking at Dae as he made his way through the club with a sneaky smile on his face.

"I'm ready to go. I told Ricky you're coming with me," he said with a look that suggested his words were a demand and not a request.

This cannot be happening, I thought. The moment was too perfect to be fully good, but I followed him out of the club and back to Ricky's car. Ricky wanted to stay longer, so he told Dae he'd ride home with a friend. We barely talked when we got in the car. Power 99FM played softly as we made our way back to Pennsauken from Philly. The short drive seemed to take forever, and every additional second caused a wave of adrenalin to race through my body. It was happening. Dae pulled into the parking lot of a diner. It was close to 1 a.m. when we arrived, but it was nearly 4 a.m. when we left. I can't recall what we talked about for three hours, but I do remember how hard we tried to start a new conversation just so we had a reason to stay a bit longer.

"You tired?"

"Nah, I'm good. Why you ask?" I responded.

I could tell Dae was more experienced than me, even though he was younger by two years. I let him lead because I didn't know how to play the game just yet, not with guys, that is. So I followed him. We ended up at Cooper River Park, a county park, five minutes from the street we lived on. During our walk around the park, I found out Dae was my neighbor. He lived a few blocks away. We continued walking as our steps traced the edges of a small pond. We shared secrets, and kisses, as the sun began to rise.

"So do you like college? I bet you fucked around with a lot of guys on campus by now, huh?"

"Nah. The last guy I messed around with lives here. But I've been fucking around with this girl named Lesley. Can you believe she got me a pair of Nikes, a Devils jersey, and pair of jeans?"

"Oh, ya shit must be real good, huh?"

"Well . . . apparently," I shot back slyly.

By the time we made it back to my house, the sun was out and my family was awake. I was nervous about them walking outside, only to see the two of us sitting on the steps, but nothing mattered to me more than his presence that day and the many days to follow.

A few months later, he ended one of our many arguments with his classic line, "You don't know how to love me." If by love he meant accept the fact he had another boyfriend while we were together, he was right. He drove to Seton Hall a few days later so we could talk through our issues. Even in my fury, I hated being away from him. A fire alarm sounded while he lectured me about my inability to give him what he needed, and I tried to convince him everything I gave him was more than I gave to myself. We kept talking as we made our way to the front of Xavier Hall, the residential hall I lived in along with the student athletes. He had on a T-shirt, boxers, and Timberland boots. Everyone stared as we argued with intensity, forgetting others were around, forgetting he was dressed in underclothes, forgetting I had tried my best to convince my peers I was straight. The night some of the other students remembered because it crystallized my diseased sexual connection to a strange black guy in boxers was, for me, one of the hardest experiences of my late teens. We were in the middle of a breakup, and I was breaking down as a result. I got what I wanted. People talked about the handsome stranger I walked the campus with. But they only saw ruins in place of beauty. I was no better for using him, for using his presence as an excuse to be brave, only to fail in the long run.

My quest to be seen as normal, as hard, as straight, nearly resulted in me losing my life. I was focused on my heart, fragile because I abused it with drugs and broken because my peers seemed to think it was strong enough to suffer a blow, while students on campus were focused on whom they imagined I slept with in my dorm room. They were partially right. I had sex with a guy I chose not to acknowledge in public, a decision I would make over and over again, sometimes resulting in hurt. The young minister friend who relayed the rumor, for instance, was one of the guys I would eventually have sex with often. I wasn't ready to openly acknowledge my relationships. Even Lesley, the girl I had sex with during my first year, asked me once after we were finished messing around, "You like dudes, too? I think you do and it's cool."

She was right, and it was her coded acceptance that I took to heart when Dae and I met, but I was also addicted to sex with her. She turned me out, as we would say then of people who have sex partners dreaming about and drooling over them in their absence. She did things with and to my body men had yet to do. In fact, the first threesome I enjoyed she arranged. She invited a caramel, brown-skinned, fit guy from Newark to join us. She seemed to enjoy the interplay between him and me. Several threesomes, orchestrated by Lesley, followed.

But none of that mattered. In the collective imagination of my peers, my body was rendered diseased in ways it has always been imagined by strangers and family members like my Aunt Cookie. In ways I, too, imagined it being. Difference, queerness, deviance is so terrifying it demands disposability and death. But it was also my magic.

Returning to campus mended could only happen if I was brave enough to piece myself back together and live once again. If I were to run this time, it would be toward, and not away from, the fight. Some fights, however, we must be willing to lose.

Chapter 6

UNBECOMING

I was stretched out on my parents' couch, overthinking. My mind was full of hard questions and calmed by an occasional answer. The night felt exceptionally long as I lay in the dark, enveloped in a loud silence.

Having so much time on my hands while home from school on medical leave meant I would lose many hours of sleep overthinking. Dae and I had broken up a few months before, and my heart and self-esteem were shattered still. Knowing a rumor, a lie, was circulating on campus about my medical condition was difficult to process. And drifting between self-acceptance and annihilation pushed me to the limits of the strength I had drawn upon for twenty years.

It wasn't that the problems I faced were so unique. I wasn't an exceptional victim of life's common circumstances. But so often those who try to manage and survive problems on their own end up caving in. The belief that we have all we need within us, individually, to survive is a powerful, poetic idea, but the truth is, no one person can make it through life alone without the presence and support of others who are willing to draw upon their own strength to aid another at their lowest. I thought my family and closest friends would be able to read my forlorn disposition and know my insides were falling apart even as I seemed to hold things together. But sometimes hurt goes unseen, and it's no fault of those around us. I too have slept while people I loved struggled.

The house was eerily quiet. I tried to mute my sobs and whispers. *Why me? I didn't choose to be gay. Why the constant teasing and hatred? And if I am gay, why didn't my relationship to the one guy I was brave enough to love on purpose end?*

Questioning parts of myself, even after having convinced myself over and over again that my sexual difference was lovable, caused me to experience a type of existential schizophrenia.

I was of two minds, torn apart by two inherent beliefs— an awareness of my human worth and a denial of my sexual difference. I struggled to affirm and love the parts of myself I rejected and hated. In a world where black people are taught to covet whiteness and riches and gender conformity and traditional family structures and perfect bodies and heterosexuality, we must fight like hell to unify all aspects of our personhoods that have been ridiculed and rejected. Loving oneself and being loved while navigating the violence that harms black people's psyches and well-being is a survival tactic that requires work. Staying alive when you've been counted dead is love.

Love does not mean the pervasive grip of social, economic, and personal conditions in our lives will loosen. The longer I remained at home, away from the cloistered world of abundance I encountered outside Camden, the more aware I became of the ways in which my family navigated life with less. Love was our currency, but we needed actual money to keep the lights on and food on our table. My parents, like so many of my neighbors, worked harder than most to obtain the necessities I took for granted on my college campus. After I depleted my meal plans eating too much KFC on campus and wasted my residual student loan money on clothes, after I would steal food from the cafeteria or eat peanut-butter-and-jelly crackers when I was broke and hungry, I too realized how important it would be to finish school so I could bring my family a bit closer to the edge of abundance. But I couldn't achieve my goal as long as my heart felt like a volcanic fire set to erupt at any moment. The burdens of dislocation, unhappiness, sickness, and hopelessness collided at once. I failed to be the fabled, responsible, and straight black man, the patriarch, who was expected to hold life together in the midst of chaos.

God, I can't do this. I held a bottle of nitroglycerin pills in hand. I didn't know if ingesting a handful of the tiny pills doctors prescribed to treat the piercing chest pain I was experiencing would do the job, but I was committed to taking as many as I needed to kill myself. Somehow writing those words now, while recalling the unshakable pain I felt in that moment, almost minimizes the real-time emotional toil. Writing about it now feels too theoretical, too poetic, but self-destruction is material, overwhelmingly felt, and embodied. There are no perfect words to describe what happens when the spirit is so depleted it no longer feels any sting, when the mind is so overcome by thoughts the person can no longer distinguish reality from fiction, when all words of encouragement offered to lift you go unheard when spoken. It's dangerous to step back into the desperation that festers and lurks and overwhelms and destroys. Psychic pain escapes words.

In the past, depression took shape as a cloud. Even when the sun was blazing, it was impossible to feel its warmth and discern its light, so I would try my best to give chase until I could catch a glimpse of a ray. I wish that were a metaphor.

There were many days I moved through the streets under a haze. I would walk as if in a trance, seeing no one and everything. The brightest, sunniest days were dark, and I would feel nothing and everything at once. I wanted to feel the sun's warmth on my face and be overcome by the light, but life felt cold and appeared dark. The run was endless. My body and mind were exhausted because I could never grab hold of the light. I now wonder how many black boys and men walk under dark clouds every day, hoping to appear closer to the stereotypical images of success and masculinity so many of us are taught to emulate.

It wasn't that I was too weak to simply think differently or give a middle finger to hateful people. I wanted to die, which is to say *not live*, which is to say *not have to be strong enough all the time to fight to exist*, which is to say *fight at all*, which is to say, *I really want to live without having to fight so damn hard to exist.*

There was no way I could prevent tongues, hands, theologies, or laws from doing me harm. No easy way out of compounding debt from loans I acquired while broke at eighteen to obtain a degree I thought would end generational cycles of poverty. No quick way to fix years of untreated trauma and the kind of normalized melancholy that was characteristic of many in my family who held on to hope and love when violence and economic distress hit us.

I come from a large family. My aunts and uncles, grandparents and parents, blood and play cousins rarely cried and sometimes hugged, but for the most part we contained our emotions, especially the boys and men. The unspoken rule seemed to be that one must learn to regulate one's feelings and to deal with whatever comes one's way no matter how severe, no matter how beautiful. It's a coping mechanism that probably makes sense to many black people. We've always been considered strong enough to cope with any and all afflictions. But there is no way for us to control the forces of the world that do their best work unseen—from racism and hood shaming to desire policing and economic pillaging. The weight is heavy. The body and spirit bearing that weight are not so strong that they can continue to carry the burden interminably. Death, among some, is not always conceived of as dying when you are already perceived as dead; rather, it is imagined as another way of living beyond the boundaries of others' perception; it's another way of snatching freedom. But we should not have to concede victory to death when all we really demand is a life free of psychological and material violence. When all we demand is love and love's loving consequences.

I swallowed four pills. And paused. I loved my family too much to hurt them. I didn't want them to wake up, only to stumble upon my body when they walked downstairs. I didn't want to die a weak death.

I called Ramik and mumbled, "What you doing? I think I need help." He had picked up the phone in the middle of his sleep. He muttered a few words of encouragement and hung up the phone so he could continue sleeping.

Depression caves in on you and forces seclusion. It will have you feeling like you are standing at the seams of a life, braver than ever, ready to leap closer to death while family members are several feet away but sleeping, while friends are on the phone listening but too exhausted to hear you.

I swallowed a few more pills. Pause. My back was against the sofa, and my legs were stretched out on the floor. More pills. And I paused. I continued to pray and weep until my mind stopped raging. Pause. I either passed out or cried myself to sleep because I woke up a few hours later stretched out on the floor, still alive, as the sunlight entered through our window.

It was Easter weekend in 1996, Holy Saturday, a time when Christians reflect on the limits and expansive nature of affliction and victory, of life and death. I was twenty, thirteen years younger than Jesus was when he gave up his life. Jesus was a man, albeit a divine one we are told, who sacrificed his life for the sake of redemption. *How fitting*, I thought. Christian theology is centered on the sanctity of death. A man's "flesh" must be subjected and sacrificed if he is to be free. I interpreted that literally.

My friend Warren phoned me a few hours after I woke up. Still dazed, I confessed I had tried to kill myself. He wasn't alarmed because he understood. He was a church boy and a professional musician who loved God and men. He lived with the same tensions; he had been taught his affections were sinful, and he believed God would deliver him from his desires. But neither of us yet recognized our flesh, our lusts, and our very beings were gifts. Despite the contradictions, Warren was full of love. He was younger than me by a few years, but he carried himself like an old soul. He prayed with me that morning until my eyes welled up with tears, and he promised he would support me. He did. An hour or so later, Warren drove from Cinnaminson, a short fifteen-minute ride to Pennsauken, to pick me up. I traveled back with him to his house, and I listened as he read scriptures and sang gospel songs he played on his keyboard. The next day I stood up when the pastor of his church, the Refuge Church of Christ in West Philly, invited visitors to give their lives to Christ. I did and was baptized the same day.

God had shown up. I was alive and, in that moment, I wanted to keep living. I had skipped death once, a few months before when I survived a heart attack, but I had tried my best to embrace it in those desperate moments at my family's house. I won by failing. And Warren was the divine presence, even if he didn't know it. Not all gods are invisible, faultless, presumably straight, masculine, and white.

The happenings in life that bring us to our knees are not always the heaviest weights we bear. It's possible to be so conditioned to carrying life's heavy baggage that we begin to treat our bodies as if they are coffers. Some of us learn to walk, if we can, carrying the weight, hunched over to the point that moving about with our backs firm and straight feels abnormal and painful. The deep psychic pain I experienced brought me to my knees, but God, I proclaimed, had saved me. And during the several years that followed, I poured my love into a god I worshipped while slowly denying love to myself. I returned to campus transformed, but not all transformations are good. I turned to God as a way of turning away from self, in an attempt to become a black man respected, a black man seen as normal, a black man who ended trapped inside a trope. The church did more to shore up my faulty ideas of black manhood and patriarchy than push me toward liberation from the lie of normativity. My failure to be the man I assumed others wanted me to become loomed, but some shit we fail at should be counted as a win. I didn't realize that then.

URSULA AND I MET during my first year at Seton Hall. She was from Brooklyn—East New York, to be exact. And, because context mattered in a place where the specificity of black working-class experiences was ignored, it's important to note she grew up near the projects, close to the infamous Pink Houses. She understood what it took for her to get to a college campus in New Jersey from where she came, and she was committed to not forgetting. I was attracted to her swag and fire, and related, without ever stepping a foot in Brooklyn, to her stories.

"Booga," she would say in a slow and measured drawl, "them girls messing wit the wrong one. They betta ask somebody." I'd giggle because I knew she meant every word.

Like the black girls I grew up with, she refused to break her stride. She was everything I imagined a black girl from New York City to be; a live version of the '90s Mary J. Blige, who just happened to be one of her favorite singers. A slightly oversized purple leather jacket cropped over her petite body, dangling hoop earrings, dark brown skin, a round head topped by long braided extensions, street wisdom, and a piercing look whenever peers stepped to her punctuated her presence. She was fully present in the world, and she made sure others recognized that fact. Ursula was unafraid, self-possessed, and demanding because she had to be. It matters that she was the first person on campus I came out to. It matters that she helped me survive. It matters because black girls and women had been rooting me in care and affection all of my life, even when I didn't provide the care and affection they may have needed from me.

The queer magic I possessed, which I assumed distinguished me from straight black boys, didn't prevent me from relying on the bad powers of male dominance. School locker rooms, barbershop conversations, some of the '90s hip-hop songs I loved, and church sermons were just some of the sources that informed my thinking about manhood. I learned to accept the women- and femme-despising ideas perpetuated by so many people and institutions around me because they proved to benefit me even as patriarchy violently impacted the lives of the women in my life I loved, like my mother. In many ways, I was no different than the black men I hated for hating me. We were of the same tribe and mind.

Black girls are expected to mother black boys who are and aren't their sons, and black boys, queer or straight, often demand our mothers, sisters, friends, and partners meet and even exceed that expectation. All boys are taught that the world is theirs. But black boys learn early on that the world they are required to rule is the home—the place often sustained by the visible and invisible labor of black women and girls we share homes and relationships with. The home is likened to a kingdom black boys are expected to provide for, fight to protect, and lord over. Outside the home, the streets black boys navigate are controlled by the state and the wealthy, and black boys' freedoms are restricted and policed.

White boys are raised to rule the home, the streets, the banks, the courts, the legislative halls, the church, the academy, the medical industry, the military, and the country. They are granted permission to travel through the world never questioning their need to control others' bodies and properties, never reflecting on their incessant demand for respect and entitlement, never removing themselves from the center of the public imagination. Black boys are taught to replicate the white boy game, but eventually they realize the game was never set in their favor. Some then do all they can to manipulate the contest by trying to beat the game masters in a match best forfeited. If the country cannot be ruled, the home damn sure can, which includes attempts at ruling the lives and bodies of our mothers, sisters, partners, nieces, and aunties. I've played the game over and over again and have wounded black girls and women, like Ursula, in the process. I wounded myself not realizing that patriarchy—male dominance—takes aim at girls and women, and the humanity of men, too.

Unlike my sisters, I was allowed to roam the streets without much restriction. I was the first male grandchild of nearly fifty grandchildren and was upheld as a man of the house even as a boy. The freedom to fail, the freedom to fuck (girls), the freedom to escape home and responsibilities, the freedom to chase freedom—all that had come without invitation. When Ursula would write me letters and sit me down to help me understand how I used emotional manipulation to get what I wanted from her, whether money I never paid back or empathy I failed to return, I listened to her critiques. I rarely changed my behavior. *As long as I wasn't a clone of my dad*, I thought, *there was no need for her to complain*. Whatever I gave would always be much more than he ever did. I hadn't yet realized I was his son, his likeness, an ellipsis extending his presence in the world. At the time, I didn't think I needed to change my behavior because I never felt the need to apologize for actions I thought were normal.

Ursula helped me to discover the knots in my heart and mind. She realized I was listening but not changing. I thought it was okay to receive care even when I refused to give it back. Only after reflecting on my parents' relationship, specifically my father's destructive behaviors and my mother's pain, did it occur to me that I had no right to criticize a man whose ways I had begun to model. I realized, for instance, my relationship to my college crush Lesley was one of selfish convenience. I treated her like a body without a soul. I wanted physical pleasure, emotional coddling, and the benefits that came with our connection—the sex, clothes, sneakers, presence, and food when I needed them. I didn't have any desire to do the emotional work necessary to be anything other than a polite but still manipulative user. I regret hurting the girls and women who loved me then and love me now. I thought that acknowledging my errors was the ultimate goal, but naming my wrongs is not the same as working hard to undo them. I work every day to not harm, control, and use the women in my life. I try my best to mother myself. I try my best not to rely on them to mother me by being as real as possible about the work I have yet to do on myself. It took some time to realize how entrenched my issues were and are.

I was in my late twenties when it became clear to me that my quest to be different from my father was grounded in the selfish desire to prove I was better than him. A few years after, I began to understand that I needed to work on myself, change my ways, fail, and try again, because my behaviors damaged my friendships with the women in my life. The self-ish ambition to outshine my dad was not enough to spark self-transformation. Collective care, reciprocity, and love are the forces that reshaped my understandings and actions. And self-reflection was key to a long, everyday process of internal transformation.

In my quest to shed any semblance of queerness, any sign of difference, I tried to live out the image of the "real man" that was the source of my internal turmoil throughout my younger years. I tried to be hard, resistant to feeling, in control, an expert in bed even as I suffered through the loneliness that haunted my mind. I feared others would think of me as the epitome of failure. The anxiety fueled by my want for acceptance was also at the heart of my deep sadness. I really believed God would make me right. I relied on God to heal me in the same way I relied on my mother for incessant care, my sisters because of their overprotective concern, Ursula's always-available empathy, and Lesley's gifts. God was mother, and the women of the churches I attended were his divine embodiment. And I felt at peace in most of the churches I attended, when I wasn't castigated by some preacher rebuking homosexuality, because the church, like the home and women's bodies, was a site I had been taught to dominate. The churches I attended, in fact, reinforced, not abated, my attraction to patriarchal rule.

On Saturday mornings, Ursula and I would travel to Mt. Olive Baptist Church in Hackensack, New Jersey, where we would attend weekly prayer gatherings. Middle-aged black women like Ursula's older cousin, Angela, would fill the pews in the sanctuary. Angela would pick us up, and as we drove along the Garden State Parkway we would share stories, offer support, and lose ourselves in the ecstatic energy we believed was spirit as gospel music played in the background. "God is good," we would repeat in response to every testimony of personal triumph we might have experienced the week prior. Prayer service was a needed distraction from depression. It was a temporary replacement for the therapy sessions I should have had but didn't. I was convinced it was my sins that brought on the sadness and fury. After a few months of attending, I was called upon to lead prayer. My words were always penetrating, convincing, and affirming, but they were also self-loathing. The group would respond with affirming shouts of "Amen," and some attendees would weep. But they didn't know my hands, often lifted in their air, were tied.

They may not have realized my ardent faith would crumble a bit every time I prayed to be made right and continued to do wrong because I felt most human and whole when doing so. They didn't know that before and after prayer services, where some older "saints" would offer encouragement by reminding me that God would send me a wife, I would return to my dorm room lonely and horny—so I would log into gay chat sites in search of a fling as a temporary fix. But what if they did know? What if they saw in me that which I didn't see in myself? What if they loved me despite the love I lacked? Or what if they confused their quiet disavowal of my difference for love? Either way, they accepted me.

I was no more fervent or faithful than Ursula, but most of the churches I attended throughout my life had a penchant for attracting and elevating black men to visible positions of authority despite the obvious fact that black women were the anchors for pastors and their congregations. Ursula faced her own set of struggles, but she wasn't having sex. I was. She didn't split herself into two versions of a person—a sinner and saint—to save face. I did. She didn't condemn people using scriptures others had recited to condemn her. I had. She was a young black woman, which meant others saw her as a helpmate. They, however, saw me as a shepherd.

IN 1998, I JUMPED headfirst into campus ministry as director of the university's gospel choir. Some of my friends welcomed my transition into a black man who seemed to possess both charisma and a love for God. Friends would tell me God was with me. Some would constantly remind me I had a calling, a purpose God would use. After years of searching for affirmation, of both the fullness of my personhood and the necessity of my existence, I almost felt close to normal. To be seen as upright and worthy, to be seen as a black man deserving of respect, to be seen and not ignored, helped to bring me out of the hiding places collectively created by those who fear what can happen when our accepted truths are revealed to be false.

I didn't create or lock myself in a closet. Our society's idol, the god that is heterosexuality, is a closet meant to keep the power of self-creation and determination out of the hands of the brave. We stay locked away peering and snickering at anyone who escapes, and when we come upon fugitives we rush to drag them back in because we want to maintain the comfort and safety that result from their discomfort and harm.

I wish I had known that then. I wish I hadn't been addicted to the praise others showered upon me because I leapt into the depths of a shallow faith. My wounds ran too deep to be cured because people loved what I allowed them to see: a man in pursuit of patriarchy's riches. I feared revealing the innermost parts of a self I knew would cancel out any visions of my perceived virtue. I had yet to believe all of me was lovable. I learned to live a lie or, rather, I did my best to kill my desires for men and sex, for the pleasantries of young adult wonderment and debauchery, by forcing them underground.

I'm certain other students thought my transformation was strange. Some of them told me so. I was the student who once helped throw college parties, chugged liquor, smoked weed, acted tough, bragged about sex with girls, and snuck around campus with guys. They couldn't understand why I was now a Jesus fanatic, perched behind a bully pulpit, admonishing the same people I had rolled with in my past to do better. I wanted to yell loud enough to drain out the noise of my past and present hypocrisy. I wanted to rid my mind of its demons so that I could once again stand before my fellow gospel choir members and act as if I hadn't lost sleep the night before after having sex with the co-director of the choir.

Our peers thought Justin and I were "brothers," but we were much more than that. He would show up in the room along with the other choir members, and we would pretend we hadn't kissed, bickered, had sex, and lamented after all was done. We would leave campus together physically drained after teaching songs and trying our best to inspire others. And we would return to his dorm room or mother's home in Newark, where we would release our anxieties through sex. We never used a condom. We didn't care about cleanliness. What we did sometimes felt like lovemaking. But most of the time we didn't need to feel love to have sex until we couldn't feel the dissociative trauma that would return as soon as we woke up in his bed. In the morning, we would walk downstairs to the kitchen, where the rest of his family was gathered. *Back to normal*, we thought. But there was no way his mother didn't hear the squeaky bed and percussive moans.

When I didn't sleep over at Justin's house in Newark, I would return to campus where I danced between multiple sex partners, one of whom was my schoolmate and a minister who told me about the rumor circulating on campus when I was home on medical leave. Freddy seemed to love what the church signified more than he loved himself—at least, that's what I gathered during our interactions. In his church, in his position as a leader, he moved with an air of authority and respect that allowed him to silence the hushed guesses his sexual lusts may have provoked. He had a girlfriend. She was churched. And his swag was marked by his machismo. Behind the closed doors of the spaces we shared, the beloved patriarch rushed to let down his guard. *I want you inside me*, he would say before we had sex. *Brother, can you pray with me?* he would say as soon as we were done. We served two gods, our lusts and our shame. And like a repetitive scene in a tragic romance movie, I would cup his hands and together we would mourn the genuineness of our intimacy by lying to ourselves and our God. It was clear from our regular returns to our secret place, however, that we also felt pleasure was a gift we deserved to have. It had to be. Why else would it bring both of us to our knees after each encounter?

MY KNEES HIT THE linoleum floor of the campus music room, my hands were folded in front of my face, blocking the brightness of the lights, and penitent words fell from my lips. I was alone, unmasked, and disarmed in God's presence. My only connection to the world outside the room was the always-locked windows offering a glimpse into the darkness outside. *Use me*, I pleaded, *in spite of my failings*. In that same room, when it was full of mostly black students who found solace and support among community, I would stand upright and admonish my peers to live righteous lives, to renew their minds, to turn away from sin, and to be examples of God's love. But now, on my knees and alone in prayer, the words I had preached haunted me. How could I profess words I failed to follow?

Help me, God. Help me to be better. Help me to live right. I still believed my skin, my bones, my hands, my eyes, my feet, my penis, my heart, my desires, and my flesh were dirty and needed to be purified. All had been touched by yet another man I secretly loved. My longings weren't wrong, but I denied them as if they were. The theology I accepted, the idea that I must subdue my most human desires in pursuit of divine perfection—even it meant self-deception—was wrong.

I had gotten used to the newfound admiration. Some Christian communities believe that men, however righteous or damaged, are the natural leaders of the church and the home, so they give us opportunities to represent the congregation. My community had chosen me. Finally, I had landed a win in the game. If my peers refused to accept me because my brand of hood antics was too dramatized to be legit, or if they turned their heads because my attraction to men was too excessive to be cast as normal, then I would reinvent myself into a black man worthy of their respect. I would become clay in God's hands. My prayers were the fire lighting the kiln.

I had been there before. A few months earlier, I found my way into a random church in Newark and fell to my knees. I was prepared to take jabs at my soul in the name of a stern God, a father who demonstrates love for his creation by demanding they submit to punishment. And if they are unsuccessful, the punishment he will mete out is eternal separation from his love. I bent before a God who is the judge and the warden holding the keys to liberation, who seems to have always benefited the masters and never the enslaved. I've been remorseful before, when I convinced myself my wrongdoings would determine the extent to which I would be loved or not. I had been there, broken before God after I had broken the rules that should not have been in place at all. The church had harmed me more than it healed me, but I stayed because I had become attracted to self-debasement. I stayed on my knees. The church seems to prefer those believers who move about in degradation, never those journeying forward with heads held high.

I had attended a revival at a church in Newark a few months prior to being in the music room. I knelt in the dim light that penetrated the gothic stained-glass windows. On my knees, I prayed the same prayer, and shed tears. I was not alone, but I was lonely.

The visiting preacher organized a prayer line. The repentant souls took our places in line, ready to be ushered into an ecstasy of the spirit. I was desperate to rid myself of the fire within. No more sex with men. No more loving men. No more jerking off, wet dreams, chat lines, threesomes. No more deception. No more sadness, shame, mental exhaustion. If God heals according to our faith, as I was taught, then surely God could make me into the man I willed myself to become.

I closed my eyes in expectation. The preacher placed his heavy hand on my head. The sweat on my forehead mixed with the holy oil, and both mixed with my tears, as he prayed fervently into a microphone. *I rebuke the demonic spirit of homosexuality terrorizing this brother's life.* My eyes were still closed, but I was no longer raptured. I was aware that everyone in the packed sanctuary now knew the secret I hadn't shared with anyone. Was it my dress or demeanor, or was it his discerning eye that moved him to say aloud what I had wailed in silence? *Get out of him, demon!* I fell to the floor and felt several pairs of hands on my back. I ended up under a pew with thick spit foaming from my mouth. A mind tortured by hate can produce haunting effects on the body. The only demon in that place was the psychological deception cloaked under the guise of Christian love. The prayers continued. *He will walk in his purpose. He will live according to God's will. He will be free,* the preacher uttered. But I thought I already was.

My prayer went unanswered, which is why, a few months later, I fell to my knees and prayed some more in the campus music room, begging for deliverance from homosexuality. A few minutes before my friends began to fill the room, I got up from the floor, bearing a rugged cross, leaving my secrets and shame in the place my body had been. My back was straight. My head was held high. And my confidence returned. I was now the man with a microphone on the other side of disgrace, acting as if I hadn't spent twenty minutes warring with my perceived inadequacies.

The thirst for power leaves the spirit arid. That is why some of the most well-known, most beloved preachers often live the most complex, fragmented lives. Sheep desire shepherds because of the feigned faultlessness they stage. These shepherds can hurt the sheep, and even admit it when they do and still be accepted. So many lead double, and triple, lives without doing the work necessary to heal the internal brokenness they point out in others. The pulpit, and the sermon, can be weapons of manipulation and control. Those weapons hurt me, but I also benefited from their use. People thanked me for helping them to find Jesus while I raged internally because Jesus seemingly failed to find and rescue me.

But not all was lost. Whenever I would rise from the low place I was used to inhabiting, I would fall into the many extended arms of a community of young people who struggled, like me, to make sense of their worlds and selves.

I was more committed to serving alongside my peers than to finishing school. The choir members lifted and supported me. And, as I would later learn, they knew more about my secrets than I imagined. Years later, one of my closest friends, Dinean, confessed she knew Justin and I were intimately involved. She told me that the knowledge enabled her to accept her "flaws," her attraction to women, and later name it a gift. The presence of friends like Dinean, and brothers like Andre and Quentin, young black women and men who loved me whether I debased myself while my body hugged the ground or when I stood a bit taller after, is the reason I managed to navigate those years. Quentin was the first straight black man whose response to my confession of sexual fluidity was a simple "I love you, regardless." I loved him, too. They loved God, but the God they loved was the God in each of us.

I survived Seton Hall because of them, but I had no interest in attending classes or writing papers. I was ready to move on, yet again, and live unbound. I finished school ashamed of my 2.1 grade point average, but I finally finished in 1999, leaving behind a lingering tuition bill but hopeful for what was to come. When I left, I got on my knees to give thanks. I was finally prepared to live fully human. I had realized that the process of unbecoming the right kind of black man would not kill me. No. It would be the road to unflinching liberty, good love, a livable life, and a more human self. I didn't know my return to the place I ran from, my return home to Camden, would be the reason. Such is the power of the journey. Such is the power of the internal magic so many black queer and trans people summon during our many travels. Such is the power of the kind of self-affection that shows the erased their truest reflections. Such is the power of self-determination.

Chapter 7

RETURN

I left my parents' house and disappeared into the night alone. The movement of my bones, and the twisting of the sinew holding them together, made me feel alive. I wasn't dead. My flesh and desires weren't either. I wandered through the dark, shadowy blocks of Thirteenth Street, the gayborhood, in Philly. The only prayer I offered as I walked was an appeal for safety. No prayers for deliverance from homosexuality and no pleas to God for strength to resist what felt most natural that night.

Curiosity had brought me out of hiding. I wanted to feel the electric sensation of physical attraction as it moved through my body. I was ready to trade flirtatious stares and coded conversations with the strange guys I would come across while roaming the streets alone. But I didn't hook up with anyone, and I didn't drink. I walked slowly, cautiously, and watched black men command the streets, touch, sneak away into bars, talk loudly, vogue, and unbind themselves from restrictions. I knew one day I would either be totally free of my need for the same or give in completely to my urges. That night, however, I counted my ability to head home without the loaded guilt, which tended to ride my conscience after I had sex with men, as a win. I was taught that my thoughts—my visions of hands gripping hands, of lips tasting ears, of sweat mixing with sweat—were sinful, but I convinced myself to believe the act itself was far worse than the vision. I dreamt a lot while awake.

As I walked back to the subway, I smiled in awe of the person I was becoming. Every second I spent alone on Thirteenth Street was necessary. I needed to know that freedom looked like black queer and trans people fully present in their bodies, unashamed, and alive. And I needed to know black joy was as palpable as the shared pain that comes from societal rejection. I felt a spark of happiness and self-love that night. It was late, a little after 2 a.m., and I wanted to get home while the buses and trains were still running from downtown Philly to Camden. If I was brave enough to sleep on the streets, amid the free people who seemed to care more about life than other people's opinions, I would have stayed forever just so I could be caught up in the magic.

But I had to head home because I didn't want my family to worry. I had already stayed away from home as much as I could just so that I could live as I pleased. Every day, I drifted farther away into my secrets. My mom told me several years later that after my return from Seton Hall, she knew I was keeping to myself because of my need for self-preservation. My sister Tasha also confessed that she and my sisters had read my love letters and were aware of my attraction to men. They knew I carried secrets. I hid a more honest human self behind the good Christian persona I performed because I hoped it would address others' perpetual questions about my intimate life. I figured they'd interpret the absence of a girlfriend as a sign of my allegiance to faith and God, and leave me alone to dwell in my wonderment. "Soon God will send along a wife," I would say, "but right now my focus is on myself and my calling." But when I disappeared into the night, sometimes alone, I walked the streets in search of the life I wanted to lead.

Walter Rand Transportation Center in downtown Camden is the kind of place most people stay away from in the middle of the night. It wouldn't be too long before a person, possibly homeless or high, would come along asking for money or other favors. I hadn't lost my street smarts so I knew to place my wallet somewhere on my person and stash my jewelry in my pockets to avoid being pickpocketed. It was a quiet night, the kind of night that provoked caution, but I waited patiently for my bus.

A car pulled up.

"You need a ride?" the man asked. The driver's side window was rolled down just enough for him to stick his head out.

It was a common ask. Hacks, as we called them, sold rides in personal vehicles used as makeshift taxis. The voice was familiar, but I couldn't make out the man's face.

"Where you heading? I can take you."

There were no buses in sight. It was late. And I was tired of waiting. I walked to the car to check things out before I got in. I wanted to be sure I wouldn't have to fight my way out of a robbery. I had been robbed, once at gunpoint, many times before. I moved closer and realized it was him. His chestnut-brown skin, chubby face, heavy eyes, and cool swag I would forever remember. I knew those rough hands and remembered his scent, which smelled of long days spent outside. My father, Grafton, whom I hadn't seen or heard from in several years, had appeared serendipitously in the midst of my secret journey.

Encountering my father was like running into a ghost. I rarely saw him after my mom finally broke it off with him when I was fourteen. To say I hated him would only reveal a surface truth. I hated my need to be loved by him. And I hated the way my heart opened in his presence because I knew he wouldn't enter even if invited. I tried my best to disconnect my spirit from my body. I didn't want to feel warmth or joy. I just wanted to get home without being let down.

"Son? Son! Get in the car. I'm taking you home."

I opened the passenger door and got in. The last time I had been this close to him was years earlier, when I watched police officers drag him off to jail after he tried to kill my mother. I tried to avoid his gaze in hopes I could also dodge any questions he may have had regarding my whereabouts. I was his son and a stranger, but in my mind I played out the conversation I wanted us to have.

"Where are you coming from this late?" he'd ask.

"Well, if you really wanna know, I was chillin' on Thirteenth Street in Philly. We haven't talked in years so you probably have no clue I'm gay," I'd respond, as nonchalantly as possible.

And without hesitation, he'd look over at me, stare directly into my eyes, and say, "Next time you want to go, tell me. I'll go with you so you won't have to go alone."

That's what I hoped he would say. An hour earlier, I had been roaming the streets open to the possibility of connecting with a man, any man, bold enough to challenge me to let go, and strong enough to let down his guard to hold me. And now I had arrived back in Camden and found the man whose return I had been waiting for.

He was the first to break the silence. "Son, I'm so proud of you. You finished college. I've been telling everybody my son graduated."

"Really? Yeah, I did it."

What I really wanted to know was where he had been. I wanted an explanation for his absence and nonexistent apology. I focused my eyes on the road, consumed by flashes of pain followed by hurt followed by anger and shame. There was nothing he could say that could take the place of a simple "I'm sorry." Was he not aware that I spent many nights trying to figure out the reasons he didn't call or write or send me money or tell me I was missed? Did he forget what I could not disremember? His hands pounding my mother's body, holding a crack pipe, crushing the backdoor window of the house we shared so he could break in? And the ways he bragged about me, the time he stood bare before me in the bathtub, the time he kidnapped my youngest sister and left her alone in some stranger's house? He talked as if we were good, squared away, as if time hadn't elapsed. And I refused to look him in the eyes because I tried my best to push back the love and need for him that intensified every long second it took for us to get to my house.

I feared every man who would come into my life after him would abandon me without explanation and cause. The wall I had constructed around my heart was not of my design. I built it because of him and his absence. I sought touch and affirmation because I was perpetually chasing someone who could fill the void he had left in my life. And the many versions of a man I tried on had everything to do with my attempt to be a different type of man than he was. I didn't want to look him in the face because I feared I would face my own reflection. As long as he figured as the antagonist in my distorted imagination, I could go on feeling better about my own failures. I hurt those who loved me. I lied, too. Anger suited me well. I summoned my rage as a form of protection. I was tempted to forgive him, but doing so would have stripped me of the only weapon I had mastered.

We arrived at my house in less than ten minutes, though it felt like hours. I looked through the passenger window at my house, waiting desperately for him to apologize. Maybe if he makes his move, I thought, all will be well with me, with us.

"It was so good to see you, son. You only have to give me ten dollars for the ride," he said without a pause.

Silence. And then I looked at him while trying to figure out how to respond.

"Wait, what did you say?"

"Just ten dollars. It will help me out."

I reached in my pocket and gave him whatever amount of money I had. I said goodbye and left the car with a heart more calloused than it was before we had our brief encounter. I never asked my father for anything. Not love. Not time. Not money. He was the adult parent, and I expected him to do the work to make amends, but he only widened the breach. How could he brag about my graduation without acknowledging his lack of contribution to my achievement? How could he fix his mouth, and firm his heart, to ask me for cash for a ride home in the middle of the night? Why did I hold in the fire I had released upon so many people who loved me and allow him to walk away unsinged?

Years later, I understood. He had been ensnared in a web of guilt. I figured the longer he spent trapped within a mind consumed by thoughts of all he had done wrong, the easier it was for him to cope. His silences were a consequence of dodging the memories he knew would eat at his strength. Like father, like son, I realized. Dre died a short time before my return home from college without receiving a proper apology from me. I had slept with the man he loved and only confessed after someone else had broken the news to him. For years, I thought about calling him and pouring out my heart as I begged for forgiveness, but I had found comfort in my silence and guilt. My silences did not encourage Dre to forgive me. They didn't help me to confront my selfish behavior. My silences didn't correct the crack in our friendship; they exacerbated the heartbreak and allowed me to make excuses for my actions. I assumed my father thought his presence, without a real conversation confronting our complicated past, would move us forward in the same way I thought my silences would bring Dre and I closer. But death reached Dre before my humility did. I continued to suffer, much as I imagine my father did on our drive home that night.

I was home, and returning home required a series of confrontations with my secrets and the people who shaped me. If I were to grow into the person I was set to become, I would need to grapple with my fears and my relationship to the city where I first learned what it takes to survive.

I WAS BACK IN Camden because I had no other choice. I had graduated and hadn't gotten any of the dream jobs I'd applied for. I had been home at my parents' house for only a few weeks when I encountered my father. A short time after my encounter with my dad, I joined a group of twelve young adults selected as "urban youth missionaries" who committed several months to a year to a ministry and nonprofit organization that was a spin-off of the Evangelical Association for the Promotion of Education named Urban Promise.

I was provided a thirty-dollar-per-week living allowance, health care, and a place to live. It wasn't enough to survive, but my family supported me when they could as they always had. I was humbled, if not crushed, by my inability to do what I wished. Gone were the days of my return home from college when I would wear new clothes and sneakers I purchased on maxed-out credit cards and student loan reimbursement checks just so my family would believe the first person to obtain a degree from a four-year college had made it. I couldn't afford to buy my sisters hoop earrings or surprise my mom with expensive purses. My family was proud and bragged about my accomplishment, but I never told them I was in debt because of the bills I accumulated when I was hospitalized. They didn't know I graduated and obtained my degree in principle only. They didn't know I never held my actual bachelor's degree in hand because I could not afford to pay off the five-figure amount I owed to Seton Hall upon graduation. I would go on to receive two more graduate degrees I would frame, but I still have yet to receive my undergraduate degree to this day. I needed to return home to remember black people are not somehow bettered by achieving the American dream. Instead, we are sometimes disillusioned when we discover the gods of our American fantasies bestow favors sparingly. My hard work and achievements, the fact I succeeded despite the threat of death and self-destruction, carried me no farther than the place I began. But my return home changed the trajectory of my life and shaped my vocational path.

I barely slept the first night in the new home I shared with twelve other urban youth missionaries. Or the second. Or the thirtieth. After I'd enter the bedroom that smelled of warm sweat and hard sleep, I'd change into my pajamas and quietly climb into my twin-sized bed with dread. I followed the same routine every evening of my six-month stay. I'd tuck myself under the covers until I imagined I was alone and not sandwiched between two strangers, bury my head under my pillow to drown out the noise emanating from the bed of my Scottish roommate, whose snores outdid the intensity of his speaking voice, and then fall asleep after pondering how I ended up sharing a room in Camden with a brash Scottish bloke and a low-key white Californian dude.

Never before had I shared a bedroom with two white people for more than a night or two. And I was terrified. Peering into mirrors—the eyes of other black people, even if they are strangers—requires less work. It feels safe. But staring into windows—into the lives of those who exist outside the worlds black people knew and inhabited, as poet Lucille Clifton once remarked—is work that tests the limits of one's grace and hospitality. It's risky work, too. If I knew nothing else, I knew black people to be gracious. Growing up, I could always locate semblances of myself in the worlds black people conjured and moved about in. The subtle gaze or nods other black people offered me in the presence of masses of white people signaled our connection and an awareness of each other's presence.

I had built friendships with white students during my years at Mullica Hill Friends School and Seton Hall University, but I never visited their homes or shared any space more intimate than cafeterias or campus grounds. I always assumed my friendships with white people weren't safe because the white friends I had never extended invitations to their homes and I didn't invite them to mine. But my two white roommates had made Camden a temporary home. Of the thirteen volunteers, twelve were white and from cities far from Camden. I wanted to know why they had come, and I spent many hours awake at night puzzled by their motivation.

It was 1999, and I was twenty-three, but I still didn't believe white people, even the well-meaning ones, could reach beyond their stereotyped perceptions of black people to see us as anything other than lesser humans in need of white saviors' preferential help, especially the black working-poor people in Camden my white missionary peers had presumably come to serve. My relationships to white people were minimal and never extended beyond the peripheries of their lives, so I'd often wonder about the everyday happenings in white people's worlds beyond what I had read in every literature and history book I was provided during my schooling. What did they eat for dinner? Did they sit around a dinner table or eat wherever they could find a place in their homes? And speaking of homes, did they rent or own or inherit their properties? Did they live in housing projects and get harassed by police if they were young and loud and free?

I always wondered about those things. Even the few white people I met during my childhood in Camden carried themselves as if their economic scarcity was balanced by the sum of their whiteness—at least, that is how I saw them. Whether they purchased groceries from the same corner stores black people did or used the same color-coded books of food stamps as their black neighbors, their brand of poverty appeared less abject and amoral. If white people were deemed poor, the problem was not inherent or a consequence of their personhood. They were considered outliers, the city's "poor white trash," because they ostensibly failed to make good on their whiteness, the promissory note ensuring their social and economic ascent in America.

I resented my white peers at Urban Promise at first. Black people in Camden didn't need any help from white people who could swoop in temporarily from the comfortable places they would later return to when their services reached their end. But it later occurred to me that some of my anger had less to do with them. I had finally graduated after barely making it out of college, and unlike my black college peers who went off to well-paying corporate jobs or graduate degree programs, I returned home no more "advanced" than I was when I left. What was the point of damaging my credit and overburdening myself with loans I couldn't pay back and working so hard not to fail out of school if the payout was a deduction in hope and money? Where was my American dream?

But every time I walked from the house I shared with my fellow missionaries to my parents' house, I was reminded of why I needed to come home. I had almost forgotten about the broken and uneven slabs of cement sidewalk, the boarded-up homes left abandoned after foreclosures, the stray dogs, the shattered glass lining the edges of streets, the trash-filled sewage drains, and all the many conditions those of us who called Camden home built families and lives in spite of. Over breakfasts I shared with my twelve ministry peers, we discussed the spectacular display of economic disenfranchisement and political neglect that rear-ended the collective hope of Camden residents. When I walked through my neighborhood, I saw it with a new set of eyes. I navigated streets I'd grown up on with white people whose understanding of poverty had come by way of an exercise in cultural immersion, Christian sympathy, and white salvific guilt. And I began to accept Camden for what it was: a home that had long ago been deemed too black, too poor, too hood, and too hopeless to be reimagined and redeveloped.

The shock my peers expressed was not exceptional. They had come to discover what those of us who called Camden home had always known: we had been willfully forgotten. If white people and moneyed black folks could not be convinced to move into southern New Jersey's slum, there would be no reason to fix a city that had long been broken because of political negligence. It appeared as if the tears of lament that fell from my peers' eyes moved others to feel. Their prayers, their pleas, and their rage caused others to take heed of the neglect. Why else was Urban Promise able to buy and develop many properties, ship white missionaries to Camden from around the world, lease vans, and start a school, if not by convincing donors to give money based on white people's testimony?

We traveled to churches in the suburbs to tell the unique stories of Camden youth and families we served as if Camden were a faraway place in a third world country. I needed to bear witness. I needed to understand more clearly what I had only partially discerned growing up. People who lived outside our city never wanted to look through the window. I needed to be home to remember my family had survived only because of the love we gave to one another. When mostly white donors gave money, out of a type of love that really resembled guilt, their hearts were not bent toward my family and neighbors necessarily. They were moved by the emotional vulnerability of other white people who claimed proximity to Camden's people and stories by subjecting themselves to the way of life in an impoverished city. Before our visits, these well-meaning churchgoers most likely assumed the black and Latino people who made lives and families and communities in Camden were perfectly fine as long as they remained there.

As part of my service, I worked as an after-school instructor providing academic support to middle-school students bused to Urban Promise from public schools across the city. I prepared snacks, planned academic enrichment lessons, came up with scripture games, and fell in love with the youth, but it wasn't exceptional work. Whenever I would come across the name of a younger cousin on our roster, however, I realized its importance. While at Seton Hall I threw myself into all manner of service focused on uplifting someone else's child, but discovering some of my cousins were reading far below their grade levels was a heavy hit to my conscience. They were my kin, and they relied on the support given by Urban Promise to achieve their academic goals.

To know the smiles of white missionaries from outside the city were fueling their encouragement pained me. How did I come to believe their well-being was not my concern? What lie did I believe that had me running as far from home as I could? Why did I want to forget what had always been forgotten? The lesson we learn about American success is that it takes individual achievement to bring about collective uplift. But if I knew nothing else growing up in the hood, I knew collective work had always been the salve for individual triumph. It was a lesson I had almost forgotten before I arrived home.

Every week, I traveled to a drug rehabilitation program in North Camden where I facilitated a weekly Bible study. Some of the men in the group resembled my father and uncles and cousins and family friends. They were battling crack and heroin addiction. Some struggled with alcoholism. I tried my best to journey along with them through bouts of sobriety, but the experience began to break me, too. Faith in God can be a powerful tool on the route to self-discovery and healing, but people can't be healed by God if they don't fervently believe their bodies and souls are also worth loving. Some would return to using and I would know it, but they would still testify about their faith in God even when they berated themselves in the same sentence. It was during that time that I found out one of my aunts, one of my mom's younger sisters, Aunt Arlene, was working though her own drug addiction. I watched her fall apart and put herself back together many times. We would communicate through letters when she was in recovery. And I would tell her what I would tell the brothers I met with weekly: you are going to be okay. Even when I didn't believe she would be, I understood what it meant to say those words again and again. I understood what it meant to be present for those we care about. Even though I still resented every rejection I received that forced me back to Camden, I was clear I needed to return home to reconnect to all that really mattered—the people and place that gave me hope despite the reality of struggle. I am grateful I returned to Camden, even if I felt forced, because had I not gone back I would not have begun to question my purpose or sought to rediscover who I really was and am.

After my short stint with Urban Promise, I started teaching at the San Miguel School, a Christian Brothers school, in South Camden in the fall of 2000. My experience as an educator was limited to my work with Urban Promise and, before that, a few summers of intensive teacher prep in Newark as part of the Kids Corp program while I was a student at Seton Hall. So I was elated when the principal, Brother Bill, took a chance and hired me. I wore a suit to my interview and my long hair was braided in cornrows. I was twenty-four and looked close in age to the students who would be under my care. Teaching was the last job I thought I'd have, but I assume Brother Bill knew I would be able to connect with the black and Latino boys in ways the older, white, Christian Brothers could not. Here was my opportunity to step up, to pay my love forward, to fill the role so that a well-meaning white missionary would not have to move to Camden to do the work I knew I needed to take on.

I knew little about pedagogy, planning lessons to accommodate the multiple intelligences of my students, or adolescent development, but I knew what it meant to grow up black, without much money, doing my best to thrive in under-resourced public schools in Camden. I knew the ingenuity it took to make it home from school without being harmed or giving in to the temptation to harm someone else.

When I looked into the variously brown faces of my students, fifteen eighth-grade boys who had either been kicked out of their previous schools or were in search of an alternative school where they might succeed, I saw myself. Thomas, a black student who struggled to write a complete sentence at the start of the school year, earnestly believed he was stupid because others, including previous teachers, had told him as much. Thomas was intolerable during my first few months. He disrupted my lessons, threw things when publicly corrected, refused to complete assignments, and regularly walked out of the classroom after slamming the door and screaming, "Fuck you!" or "Shut the hell up!" Every morning I would wake up anxious because I knew Thomas would be there, ready to put on a show. It wasn't until I noticed Thomas was sitting as far as he could from his classmates and me that I started to realize what Thomas needed. I remembered hearing a professional development instructor encouraging teachers to be most mindful of the one student who sits closest to the window, the one who appears the most distant. That student, he explained, is the one most in need of your attention, but teachers often fail to heed the signs. I had failed, too, until I remembered that I had been the one sitting closest to the window during the entirety of my college experience. No matter what I did to win the attention of my professors and counselors, nothing seemed to work.

In Thomas, I saw myself and my insecurities. Like him, I internalized the messages of failure others repeated throughout my life. By the end of the year, Thomas was writing five-paragraph essays. I'd love to credit myself for his accomplishment—I gave him more time, one-on-one instruction, empathy, and care—but I know Thomas was the source of his growth. He began to believe in himself, and his abilities, because we gave him no choice but to touch the greatness he carried within. I taught many students like Thomas during my four years at San Miguel, but I walked away having earned the education I thought I would receive in college. I entered college believing I would leave intellectually prepared for the workforce, but I graduated more curious about the world, more aware of the forces shaping my life as a black, sexually fluid man, more sensitive to the needs of black people who lacked access to the ivory tower, and more in touch with my own arsenal of intolerance. I also realized that much of what I knew I had learned first from the people who raised me.

I RECEIVED A CALL from my maternal grandfather, George, in late spring 2001. He asked me to stop by his house. He never called unless he wanted to surprise me, which was often, or to let me know there was an emergency. I was nervous. My stepfather, Lee, volunteered to drive me over. My grandparents still lived in the same house they owned on Vanhook Street, which was the house they purchased after they moved from Broadway, in the Whitman Park neighborhood of Camden. It was the same house I lived in when I was doused with gasoline. When we arrived, my grandfather was sitting in the living room. On a typical day, several of my cousins would be lounging or running around the overly furnished room, but it was strangely quiet and empty when we arrived. My grandfather was a calm man, but his silence seemed purposeful as he sat in the garishly patterned sitting chair he always occupied. I sensed he would share news I wasn't prepared to receive.

"Well, I need to tell you something. My doctor told me there's not much they can do about the cancer," he mumbled.

"What? What do you mean?" I asked.

"I have prostate cancer. And it has spread. They are giving me a few months to live, but there's a chance they can slow it down if I have surgery to remove some of it over the next week or so."

The man who was everything to me—a father, a confidante, my cheerleader, my source of inspiration, my protector—had just confessed he was about to die. Time stopped. *This cannot be happening*, I thought. I had slept at the edge of the bed my grandparents shared every night until I was about ten. At night, I would crawl into the bed as my grandparents snored loudly, a cacophonous noise that would make me laugh and keep me awake. When I woke up in the morning, my grand-father's side of the bed would be empty because he would leave early to go to the first of his many jobs. He worked so much, and so hard, that we would see him for only an hour or two each day. When we did, we would give him some space before surrounding him and engaging him in brief conversations or before we showered him with our requests for money. But his daunting workload allowed him to do things like purchase the home so many of my family members ran to when they lost their own and needed emergency shelter. No one ever suffered homelessness because Grandpop's doors were always open when we needed a place to lay our heads. Every Christmas, my thirty-plus cousins and I would sit at his feet, eagerly awaiting the white envelopes he would hold in his hand. Depending on our age, we would receive a savings bond totaling fifty or twenty-five dollars. The tuition I accrued during my time at Mullica Hill Friends, he paid off. The extra money I begged for when I wanted to go on spring break vacations or when I needed to eat and buy books, he helped to gather. Whenever my name was mentioned at gatherings, my grandfather would always brag about his smart grandson who just happened to be his spitting image. The first person in my family to tell me I had a purpose I had yet to discover—after he forced me to step behind the pulpit of the First Baptist Church of Haddonfield he cleaned and kept afloat as its sexton—was my grandfather. I'd be damned if I would allow God to take him from me when I needed him the most.

"Whatever happens to me, I need you to take care of your grandmother, Darnell."

His words hit me like bullets. He was yielding to death. And I could not bear the thought of losing him. Just weeks before, my aunts and cousins were joking about his newfound joys. They laughed at him when he would pitch a tent on the front porch of his house as if he were in a wildlife camping reserve. Our neighbors would walk by with a puzzled look as my grandfather lay sprawled out in his tent in front of a house on a densely populated Camden street where the closest thing to a tent we saw were the remnants left behind from the makeshift residences our homeless neighbors created. And then there were the tales of him riding a bike from his house to his church about nine miles away. His strange behaviors began to make sense now. He knew he was going to die, but we didn't. My grandmother didn't even know, which was precisely how my grandfather managed his affairs. He moved in stealth to keep us from being consumed with worry.

Before I left the house that day, I did what I thought I could to keep him alive. I prayed. I stood up, invited my stepfather and grandfather to join me, and grabbed his coarse, sweaty hands, full of deep lines. I looked him in the eyes and repeated with conviction a verse from the Bible I had memorized, "To be absent from the body is to be in the presence of the Lord." His body lightly jolted in response, like a somatic confirmation that his time was near. I didn't understand why I said those words, but when I closed my eyes to pray I began to cry because I knew I had just given in to the truth. I wanted to take them back, but I continued to pray for "God's will" to be done. It was finished. I knew he was leaving us. I only required the strength to carry on.

A few days later my grandfather was admitted to the same hospital I was born in, Our Lady of Lourdes, a short distance from his house. The surgery went well, but the doctors informed us the cancer was aggressive and had spread throughout his body. I began to count the days. My grandparents were young. He was sixty-seven. My mom, his second-oldest daughter, was only forty. I, his eldest grandchild, was only twenty-five. Our family hadn't lost anyone until his passing. He was the first, and we were not prepared for the departure of the quiet force whose presence, poems, prayers, and provision had kept us through days upon days of trials and rapture.

I was in Plainfield, at Justin's new house, when the day arrived. My mother phoned me, and I knew before she said anything that his time was near.

"Darnell," she said, before she paused, took a breath, and wept, "they are not giving him much time to live."

It was May 25. Justin watched as I put down the phone with tears streaming down my face.

"Pack your things. I'll drive you home right away," Justin said.

The ride along the New Jersey Turnpike from Plainfield to Camden was painful. We sat in silence as sorrowful gospel songs played in the background. I couldn't stop the tears from falling. The agony was a wound in my spirit. When we arrived at the hospital my large family, including my grandmother, aunts, uncles, cousins, great-aunts, and second cousins, were present. Everyone was despondent. The attending doctor encouraged us to pay our respects, and we entered the room like a congregation broken by the sudden departure of its shepherd. A white sheet covered grandpa's body, which was smaller and more fragile than it had seemed only weeks before. His chest moved with force, in and out, in an almost perfectly timed rhythm. And those of us who gathered grabbed hands as I prayed.

"Father, thy will be done. Receive your servant. A man who taught all of us the meaning of love. Unto your hands we commend his spirit. We won't fret, because we know to be absent from the body is to be in your presence, dear Lord."

His breathing stopped, his chest stopped moving, and the sound of an elongated beep filled the room. He transitioned. When I opened my eyes, everyone was crying, including the white nurses on staff. One of the nurses turned to us as she cried and whispered, "I've never experienced anything like this before. I've never seen someone depart surrounded by so much love. God bless you all. You are lucky."

She was right. We were lucky to have what most, even the wealthy, didn't. We were overwhelmed by the richness of love.

When the room cleared out, I fell onto my grandfather's body and wailed.

"Why did you leave me? I need you!" And I laid my head on his body, which was still warm enough for me to sense the close presence of his spirit. And it occurred to me that I would never be alone as I long as I did my best to walk in the spirit of congeniality he had fostered within me.

When I tell people that my family is the reason I am alive to this day, I am not exaggerating. Regardless of what trials we encountered individually and collectively, my grandparents, parents, aunts, uncles, siblings, and cousins always provided a reason to keep hope close. To this day, I believe that whatever powers conspired to set me on a path toward self-discovery and healing also allowed me to walk into the many closed doors I encountered after graduating so I could return to the people whose love sustained me. I also needed to be reminded my purpose was not about my selfish needs for gain and acceptance. I went home to confront everything I had run from: my father, the embarrassment I felt about Camden, my becoming, and my fear of loss. I received so much more than I would have if I had landed somewhere else, far away from the city and the people I needed the most. At home, and through them, I found me.

Chapter 8

LESSONS

I texted my mother a simple request at 6 a.m. in the morning: *Would you mind stopping by my office today? I need to talk to you.*

It was 2004 and I was the director of a transitional home for youth in Camden at the time. The night before, my partner, Shane, had told me he would no longer live in the shadows of my life. He refused to be my secret. There was no way he would continue allowing me to enjoy the pleasures of our intimacy if I refused to own our relationship in public. If it was okay for us to fuck in private, he would say, then our love was worth acknowledging. He was right.

When Shane and I lived together, my mom would phone me, Shane would answer, and I would act as if he was a homie I shared a place with and not the person I shared a bed and a life with. His family knew about me, but I was too scared to tell my family about him. Once we walked out of our house together, and our neighbor was loading clothes in a washer in the laundry room next to our house. I walked out first, not knowing Shane was a few steps behind me.

"Hey! How are you? And how's your roommate?" she asked.

"I'm good. He's good, too," I responded.

I walked to the parking lot to wait for Shane at his car and didn't realize he was walking beside me.

"Your fucking roommate? You really just acted as if I am your fucking roommate?"

Shane wasn't afraid to tell me the truth, which was one of the many reasons I was attracted to him. When I met Shane in 2004, I knew we would be together. We shared a mutual friend, Ramik, who would talk about the guy from Harrisburg who inspired him. Shane opened his first salon at nineteen. He was a businessman who knew how to make money. I assumed he would be a girly-acting hairstylist. I was only attracted to masculine men at the time. It didn't occur to me that my views on gender, my disdain for femme men, was the same as the disdain so many people showed me throughout my life. I really had yet to fully love and accept myself, which is why I refused to love and accept men who were courageous enough to express themselves as they desired.

When Ramik invited the two of us to dinner in Manhattan, I was eager to meet the friend he bragged about, but I wasn't expecting to fall for him the moment he appeared. Shane walked through the doors of the restaurant, and I gawked. He walked with a rhythmic bop and confident swag. His six-foot-plus frame was built like an athlete's, and his light caramel face, big brown eyes, manicured curly locks, and smooth vibe gave him a debonair look. He sat down across from me smelling like expensive cologne I didn't have the money to buy. Throughout the night, I looked in his eyes and studied the curve of his lips when he smiled. There was something about Shane that chipped away at the rock-solid barrier surrounding my heart, and I was determined to win his affections. We woke up together, in the same bed, the next morning. We jumped headfirst into a relationship. Ramik wasn't surprised. He told us he knew what would happen when we met. We'd have sex because we were fast, and then we'd likely become boyfriends.

There wasn't a day that went by after we met when we didn't see one another. I would leave the campus of Princeton Theological Seminary, where I was a student at the time, and spend my last bit of money to commute by train to Bayonne, where he lived with his roommate. A few months later, we moved into a townhouse in Elizabeth, New Jersey. We created a family, comprised of the two of us, shaped by the flow of genuine friendship and intimacy. But our partnership wasn't without its problems. We argued as most couples do and accused each other of cheating. I complained about his controlling personality and the ways in which he attempted to run the house and my life. He complained about some of my friends and often questioned why it was I chose to enter a second masters program, in theology at that, after already completing a masters in clinical counseling from Eastern University in 2004. All that damn schooling, he would say, but when are you going to start making money?

Our relationship was the gift I'd always wanted, the bond I had prayed for, but I wanted to keep our love private. Every night we'd eat a dinner one of us would cook, depending on who made it home from work first. He was a better cook, but he would get in late during the few nights of the week he worked as a high-end stylist at a salon in midtown Manhattan. Every other Sunday, we would drive his yellow Corvette or dark grey Hummer to the local supermarket and fill our carts with groceries from the list he'd create. We traveled to the laundromat together, took long trips to Harrisburg, Pennsylvania, to visit his family, and drank until we were tipsy at bars in our neighborhood or New York City. He managed the house and our bills. I'd hand over the little money I made to him to cover our rent, food, and utilities. But our relationship, which was dreamlike for the most part, nearly reached a breaking point.

Once, during a particularly bad fight, we were arguing outside our house and I swung at him. I didn't hit him, but the attempt was bad enough. I froze and pulled my arms as close to my body as possible. Shane was in shock, and I was embarrassed and devastated.

"You just tried to fucking hit me?" he screamed.

I cried as I apologized. It was the first and last time I attempted to physically harm a partner. And the one time when I could no longer cast myself as any different from the father I despised for the very same reason Shane was hurt and angry with me. How quickly do the sins of the father become the ways of the son? Shane eventually forgave me, but it was extremely hard for me to forgive myself. I realized just how easy it was to manifest the monsters lurking inside. I vowed never to do it again. The presence and care he provided after, even though I didn't deserve them, were indicative of his deep love for me. Telling my mom about the man who stood by my side despite my failures was the least I could do to honor him.

I watched the red status line at the bottom of my screen extend as my text was transmitted. I didn't want it to go through, but it did. My commute from Elizabeth to Camden was two hours by train, so I had a lot of time to rehearse my speech. Over and over again I repeated the words I would share as my heart pounded faster and harder. I feared my mom would reject me even though I knew my mother, who had never turned her back on me before, would understand. I knew my confession would be a gamble, and I was banking on her love. But I didn't know what I would do if the news upset her. For so long I believed I would need to carry my secret with me to my grave. I convinced myself that the matters of my heart, and the intimacy shared in my bedroom, were private, but that wasn't the case with straight people in my family. Heterosexual love was never hidden; it was hyper-visible and sometimes overbearing. I needed my mother to know that the man who picked up the phone when she called was holding me down every day, and was one of the reasons I remained alive. The love we shared was just as valid as the love shared between my aunts, uncles, and cousins and their partners.

I looked down at my phone every other minute, waiting for a response. Ten minutes after I sent the text, my mom's message finally came through.

I'll meet you at your job.

I stared at my phone screen for several minutes and the shame, embarrassment, trepidation, and self-hatred I had internalized for most of my twenty-eight years of life surfaced again. I remembered the many times I was called a "faggot." I remembered the times I had to fight my way home. I remembered the gasoline and matches, the rumors of HIV and the jokes, the warnings I heard in church and the prayers for my deliverance, the feelings of disgust that welled up when I was in the presence of femme boys, and the implicit lessons I picked up from family members who were overly concerned about the girlfriends I did or didn't have. I was certain I would break if my mother responded with revulsion, but I had made a decision to remove people, including family, from my life who refused to accept all of me. I refused to allow others to kill my spirit and happiness. And that is what terrified me the most as I was preparing to meet my mom. I was afraid of my newfound freedom. I feared the man I had become—less burdened and more committed to living a life unfettered. I feared liberation because I had gotten used to living in stealth, trying my best to survive in a cage. I knew how much I was willing to lose to fly. And I was afraid of losing my loved ones. But that morning I would face my fears whether I wanted to or not. It was time.

I made it to the office around 9 a.m. I sat at my desk, behind a closed door, with my hands folded over my eyes. I felt unease. Shane could not be only reason I was setting myself up for potential backlash, I thought. I had to convince myself that I needed to talk to my mom because it was time for me to confront the terror that had been a faithful antagonist in my life and not because Shane had forced me to tell her I was gay for the sake of his pride. I needed to talk to my mom for me, and him, but also because I knew she needed to hear my truth if we were to be any closer than we were.

My assistant phoned my office and let me know my mom was in the waiting area. I took a deep breath, stood up from my desk, walked out to greet her, and invited her into my office. I thought I was going to collapse. My thoughts were scattered as I tried to flesh out what I would say. We sat down across from one another. I panicked.

"Thanks for coming," I muttered with my head slightly lowered so that my mom couldn't look me directly in my eyes while I talked.

"Of course. What's wrong? Why did you want me to come up here?" She asked the question as if she already knew what I was about to say, almost like an invitation.

"Well, I . . . I . . . I don't know how to say it." I had practiced the script several times on the long ride to work, but the words were chained to my throat. I couldn't release them.

"What is it? Are you sick?"

"No."

"Okay. Do you have cancer?" Her question was a legitimate concern. We had lost my grandfather to cancer three years before. But that wasn't the secret I needed to share.

"No," I responded.

"What is it? Do you have AIDS?"

"Nah. I have a boyfriend."

The words flew out of my mouth too fast to catch them. And there was no turning back. She would either accept me, or I would go off to build my life, and family, without her.

"That's it? I knew that," she said with a half-laugh.

"You knew?"

"Darnell, I am your mom. You are my son. And I love you regardless. I've always known. I know that's why you stay away as much as you can."

Every word to follow was like a sledgehammer breaking down the thick walls of shame entrapping me. Her acceptance was more healing than any prayer, more uplifting than any group counseling session, more powerful than any force of hate I internalized.

"I'm so sorry for lying to you, mom."

"You didn't lie. You did what you needed to do to protect yourself. I wanted to talk to you, but I didn't know how you would respond. I didn't want to offend you, but I knew. And I waited."

I felt as if I had received my freedom papers—as if I had been imprisoned in a suffocating cell for 28 years, or 10,220 days, and my mother had come along with the keys to unlock the cage. I realized, however, I had been holding the keys all along. I merely shared them with my mother. She was there, sitting opposite me, loving me, because I invited her in. She accepted the invitation. And we both were changed as a result.

My insides were touched by a love so intensely powerful my body and spirit were literally reconfigured. I sat up straight. I lifted my head from its lowered position. I opened my mouth and smiled. My stomach filled with butterflies. My heart danced. I wanted to leap and run and scream at the top of my lungs, "I am gay as hell. And I don't give a fuck who's mad about it because my mommy loves me! And I fucking love me, too!"

All of my life I was taught to believe that single black mothers who have kids young, like my mama, were the cause of the problems in black families and the reason black boys like me made poor choices. We have been taught to believe black people, especially the economically strapped or urban or churched or southern, are backward and less progressive on issues of sexuality. I believed the lies for a good part of my life. But the day my mom, who had birthed me in a black city when she was a black girl, affirmed the full expression of my humanity was the day I decided to always put my faith in black people, even if my faith would be tested over and over again.

ON JULY 13, 2008, I gave a speech at Newark's gay pride ceremony. The weather was typical of a summer day in Jersey, humid and hot. As I looked down at the attendees from the podium that midafternoon, I felt the spirited energy that would cruise through my body when I was at a pulpit. I looked down to find Keith in the crowd. He stood there with his back perfectly straight, staring back with an affirming glance. His nod was his way of signaling I was doing okay. The words flowed. As I spoke, an older man who had been pacing between the stage and the ledge behind it stood in front of me and yelled, "Fucking faggot."

I paused, gathered myself, and kept reading. There was no way someone would feel so emboldened to yell out expletives in front of City Hall and city officials while police officers stood close by. I had to be imagining a scenario that wasn't happening. I kept going and began reading a quote by Martin Luther King Jr.

"Shut the fuck up, you fucking faggot," the man said once again.

I stared directly into his face and then back down at my words and in his face again and saw the traces of a rage I knew and once feared. It surfaced so relentlessly, and so often, whenever LGBT people, and those others assumed to be queer or trans, moved through streets and schools and workplaces and churches. It was a particular kind of rage, a spirit so pervasive it awakens the monsters within the loveliest of people. It's a rage I felt, too, which often had me going to war against myself. It was the consistent voice in my head telling me to kill myself and that I was better off dead anyway. It was the spirit that rumbled in my heart when I met other LGBT people, like Dre and Tariq, whose individual sovereignty made me jealous. The man looked at me the way I looked at others sometimes, the way OB looked at me when he tried to set me on fire. And

I decided I could either leap off the stage and whoop his ass or love the black man who had been taught to hate his reflection. I kept reading. And I chose to love him.

I had been working as the grants manager at the United Way of Essex and West Hudson in Newark for only a few months when I gave that speech. I started the position a year after I graduated from the seminary in 2007, the same year Shane and I broke up.

Earlier in the day, I had walked over to the CEO's office and peeked my head in to get his attention. I wasn't as close to Keith then as I am now, but even then I trusted him. He walked around the office like a true boss, donning tailored suits and expensive shoes, but his quiet and inviting persona made it easy to talk to him as if he were an older brother or trusted confidant.

"Wassup? Come in," he said, as he looked at me over the top of his computer screen.

"I'm not sure why I am telling you this, but I'm so nervous. I was asked to give remarks today at lunchtime."

"Okay," he said with a puzzled look, "what's the problem?"

"It's a gay pride ceremony. And it's happening in front of City Hall. I'm freaking out."

My hands were shaking as I explained why I was so anxious. It didn't even occur to me I was about to tell my boss I was gay. I wasn't sure how he would respond, but his calm demeanor surprised and comforted me. Being comfortable in my skin, loving the magical ways I loved, loving the intimacy

I shared with men, loving the freedom to share my truth with my family, was not the same as standing at a podium in front of the most prominent building in New Jersey's largest city proclaiming justice for LGBT people. I could not fathom giving a speech, however brief, in the presence of strangers, in the middle of the day, on the busiest street in the city, with a big rainbow flag waving above my head. I was courageous, and ready to fight for justice, but I needed a push.

"Why are you scared? You're a great public speaker. You give speeches all the time. What's different about this one?"

Keith knew exactly what to say most of the time. I appreciated the way he talked about the pride event as if it was normal and unspectacular, but that didn't calm my nervousness. Up until then, I welcomed the opportunity to stand before crowds large and small and wax poetic about racial justice and black politics. I didn't mind protesting and speaking up about gun violence or women's rights, but I had yet to understand what it means to practice a love inclusive of all black people.

I DIDN'T REALIZE HOW much faith I placed in the very ideas others used to wound my spirit. My treatment of, and lack of respect for, femme men, and the people I'd come across who rejected the trap of gender altogether, was not a mere consequence of simple preferences I developed based on personal tastes. My preferences, like my decision to "top" in sexual relationships, or my desire to wear certain types of clothing only, were shaped by the deeply ingrained commitments to male dominance and sexism I maintained and didn't deal with. But still I would accept invitations to speak about black life and politics—pointing my finger at others like an itinerant evangelist of a myopic gospel of black liberation—without realizing that the first, and most important, revolution I needed to push was an upheaval of the systems within myself.

I didn't want to stand behind the podium professing love for LGBT people because I knew doing so would require a definitive shift in my thinking and actions. If I were to speak, I would need to put into practice every word I professed. My understanding of liberation at the time centered on the bullets others aimed at me, the horrors I experienced. It was an individualist vision of self-ascendancy lifting me above the ugliness of society's hatred of gay people, and it had kept me alive. But in Newark that day, I was being called to profess love for femme men, butch women, transgender people, those who resisted categories of difference altogether, sex workers, queer and trans folk who lived in the projects, homeless LGBT youth, and those living with HIV. I carried the weight of responsibility, which is why I felt stunted and unprepared. Yet I accepted the challenge because I knew I'd be transformed in the process.

Keith looked at me as I sat before him beseechingly. "I'll go with you. Go write your remarks, and let me know when you are ready."

I walked back to my cubicle and scribbled a few words on a sheet of paper. I paused. I remembered why I had been invited to speak in the first place. The founder of Newark Pride Week, a lesbian sister named June Dowell-Burton, had befriended me a year before. She was unafraid, a brilliant organizer who preached black feminism, LGBT equality, black liberation, and economic freedom as if they were the tenets of her faith. In a city where black men are still imagined as the representative voices of the people, June was unflinching. She refused to let others quiet her voice or stifle her work. June had studied under black lesbian feminist Cheryl Clarke, who would later mentor me, and taught me all that she learned. If I were to speak, I would need to pay homage to the sister who was responsible for calling me out of the shadows of my self-centeredness.

As I wrote, I thought about Sakia Gunn, whose blood forever stains the sidewalk of Broad and Market Street, a short distance from where I was soon to speak. In May 2003, a man who lusted after her youthful body—a man who loathed the freedom she expressed as a masculine lesbian—stabbed Sakia to death. She was a child of Newark who was killed in front of her friends. I was still alive and needed to remember that not all LGBT people were.

I thought about James Credle, an elder black gay activist who moved to Newark from the South in the 1960s, who was responsible for organizing and harnessing the collective power of LGBT Newarkers and allies, alongside other activists like Gary Paul Wright and the Reverend Janyce Jackson, after Sakia was murdered. They were brave enough to put their bodies in the line of fire for Sakia, for each other, for me. They are a few of the leaders who founded pivotal advocacy organizations like the Newark Pride Alliance, the African American Office of Gay Concerns, and the Liberation in Truth Unity Fellowship Church in Newark. I had to honor their labor and join them in the gap.

I thought about my partner at the time, Bryan, whose love for the city he grew up in, the city he made his home as an adult, was the reason he worked so tirelessly as an advocate. He loved his home and people so much he would later take on the role of executive director of the Newark Pride Alliance as an unpaid volunteer even though he had a full-time job and other commitments to attend to. We traveled home together every night after working alongside one another in our various capacities as volunteers and organizers during the day. I was lucky enough to be in love with someone whose commitment to black people was as sweet as the kisses we shared. If I were to speak, I would be doing so because the love we shared was worth naming and fighting for.

I thought about the many trans women who were killed on the streets of Newark without the sound of the mass outrage Newarkers typically produced when non-trans people were slain in the city. Their spirits ghosted the city and would be present that day. I had to remember them. I wrote words I would speak in honor of every queer and trans organizer in Newark whose work changed me. I felt ready.

Keith and I walked the short distance from our building to City Hall. We barely talked. I tried my best to ready myself for what was to come. As we approached, I could see the makeshift stage placed directly in front of City Hall. The flag was waving from a flagpole on the left side of the stage. A few city council members were standing around, and several community members were waiting for the event to begin. I took my place on the stage next to June Dowell-Burton, Councilwoman Dana Rone (who was the first publicly identified LGBT person in office in the city's history), Mayor Cory Booker, and a few others. As always, June's remarks were powerful. And Councilwoman Rone was a political genius who knew how to whip a crowd into a frenzy. I walked to the dais holding close to my heart the memories of and love for my people, and I began to talk. In seminary, I had trained to become a minister. I never imagined I would one day stand in a public square and preach words of LGBT liberation after years of consuming and spreading dogma that insisted queer and trans people were going to hell.

Hell, as I had been taught to understand it all those years, would be full of magicians, spirit workers, lovers of the people whom love had been withheld from, and the souls of black folk disregarded in the freedom dreams of people who shot arrows at white supremacy. But the hell I knew then, the one we created as a people, lived elsewhere. It persisted in the hearts of those who believed that LGBT people, and all others who reject the tyrannical dictums of the powerful, would forever be punished. Hell was in the heart of the man who called me a "fucking faggot" while I proclaimed love for him. Hell was in my heart—the embers of patriarchy, antiblack racism, colorism, sexism, selfishness, willful ignorance, and contempt for some of my people. The work I was called to do in Newark, however, helped extinguished those flames, which is why I could look at the brother who wanted to hurt me with his words and still see the face of a black person who was not disposable. I experienced a spiritual and political awakening in that moment. I would have missed it had I given into my apprehensions and responded to that man with hatred and decided that his black life wasn't worth fighting for, too.

As I looked past him in the crowd, I repeated simple words: "We gotta love each other. If we don't love us, we won't survive. And if we don't love all of us, we can't walk around saying we are fighting for black people." Love was present in the form of black people who refused to be consumed by the fires within and without. True love removes the walls, those designed by hands that are not our own, which separate black people from one another. But black love is not cheap. We fight each other using the same weapons others have used, and continue to use, to destroy us. It's hard to resist fighting when you are under constant attack, but my comrades taught me how to resist the lure of disposability in a country, a world, that eats away at the humanity of black people every day. In Newark, I learned how to pick my battles. I also learned how to bow out gracefully when I failed.

THE NINE MEMBERS OF the Newark Public Schools Advisory Board were seated behind a large platform at the front of the room in the Board of Education's main building in downtown Newark. The room began to fill up as I waited alone on the side. I focused my attention on the bare white walls in front me. I needed to summon whatever energy I could to make it through the next hour because I knew the dialogue would be heated. I wasn't too worried because I had developed relationships with many of the power brokers in the city and had a good rapport with some of the most vocal activists. I wasn't used to being cast as an adversary, though.

I felt distressed because some of the people I once organized alongside, skilled and committed black activists I looked up to who tended to have my back, were now waiting to unleash their fury on me. The Hetrick-Martin Institute, a not-for-profit organization based in New York City whose sole mission is to create safe spaces for LGBT youth, had hired me to lead the design of the Sakia Gunn School for Civic Engagement in 2010. It was a dream gig I thought I could undertake with ease. Sakia's family had given us permission to name the school in her honor. What better way to ensure that the life of one of Newark's children, a black lesbian youth who lived with the defiant might of a warrior, remained forever etched in the consciousness of the people? When people would speak the name of the school, they would revere the spirit of a free black girl whose life had been violently snatched at an intersection where so many black girls and women before her were catcalled by men, a crossing where so many LGBT people were harassed by strangers, and the corner where so many black people were stopped by police. Every utterance of Sakia's name would be a reminder of the need for an expansive love that could cover all of Newark's people. But so often love is reserved for those whose presence does not disrupt our comforts. I was ready to disturb the comfort of those who opposed what we were trying to build.

I was skilled at public debate and on occasion would offer comments during City Council meetings. I worked alongside Mayor Booker after he appointed me as chair of the city's inaugural Newark LGBTQ Advisory Commission. I challenged the mayor when I thought he was wrong and when the community needed him to make better decisions. I railed against the mayor when my neighbors in a nearby public housing development were told they would be displaced the same day the mayor was on the campus of Princeton University giving the Toni Morrison Lectures. I had experience working in the trenches alongside a few brothers who started an organization they named Stop Shootin' Inc. as a way of curbing the gun violence plaguing the city.

When DeFarra Gaymon, who allegedly made a sexual advance toward a plainclothes undercover police officer, was fatally shot by police during the exchange in a county park in Newark, I was part of the coalition of activists who pressed the Essex County administrators to open a full investigation into the incident. We helped the county develop a commission on LGBT affairs in response. I thought I knew a thing or two about education, given my years teaching in Camden and working as the associate director of the Newark Schools

Research Collaborative, a project conceived by Rutgers and Newark Public Schools. But I was not prepared for the lesson I was soon to learn. Individual violence is easy to name and confront, while the violence committed by majority groups, institutions, and structures is harder to discern and undo.

The meeting began, and those of us charged with the task of leading the development efforts of the proposed five new schools were told to speak to the advisory board only. By no means were we to turn to the audience and address them directly, regardless of what they said or did. My palms were sweating as I held onto my notecards. I was sure the audience would be convinced we needed a school for students wishing to learn in a safe environment, a place where their self-expressions would be affirmed regardless of their sexual identities. They were aware of the many harrowing stories told by young LGBT and gender nonconforming students about their school experiences. They knew about the bullying, the fights, and the name-calling some students experienced. I once helped organize a pizza party for a seventeen-year-old boy who was shot, after the assailant called him a "faggot," while walking down the street. Both Sakia and the seventeen-year-old gay teen were students in Newark Public Schools. I had even trained three hundred public school educators on gender and sexual difference. Many of the teachers confessed they had trouble separating their religious and personal beliefs from their teaching responsibilities. Yet I figured the rowdy group of attendees, people who on every other occasion raised black fists in salute to black solidarity and raised their voices in the face of white supremacy, would support the design of a school for some of the most vulnerable young people in our mostly black city. I was wrong.

I walked to the podium and looked ahead at the board members who sat before me. I took a deep breath and began my remarks. I told them we needed to do what we could to make sure all of our students were safe and thriving. I even shared how I, an adult with relative protections, still feared the potential of physical harm because of others' fears of my difference. If that was my truth, how much more might our youth fear for their safety? I asked.

"No! We don't need segregated schools," one attendee yelled. I continued to look straight ahead and kept talking. The noise was getting louder.

"We don't need a school for the gays or the criminals," another attendee blurted out. The board chair, a black man I knew well, looked at me with empathy and encouraged me to focus. He reminded me to address the board.

"No to the gay school," a few people began to repeat.

I couldn't contain my rage any longer. I turned to the crowd, ensuring I made eye contact with the people I knew, and yelled, "You ought to be ashamed. How dare you stand in this room and scream in protest of a school we need for some of our children."

The chairperson tried to intervene, but I couldn't stop. I was surrounded by hordes of onlookers who, like so many well-meaning people in my past, remained quiet in the face of antagonism. But my hurt was far from personal. *Americans travel so quickly to the edges of our love*, I thought. We police the borders of care, and black people know very well what it feels like to always be omitted from the democratic concern centered on white people, and to occupy a position of dereliction. Black people dwell on the edges already. And yet we too push some of our own into the abyss of indifference.

I knew people in that audience who were always vocal about issues like gun violence, charter school expansion, gentrification, and police abuse. They defended black people in Newark whenever an issue arose, but here they were seemingly demeaning black LGBT people and downplaying the violence so many LGBT people experienced daily.

"This is precisely why we need a school. Look around. Listen to yourselves. If you, the most righteous of Newarkers, are acting like this, who will protect our young people?"

I looked back at the board with an exasperated glare. I collected my notecards and returned to my seat as the crowd continued to raise their voices in protest. When I got to my seat, someone behind me asked if I needed an escort to Penn Station when the session was done.

"Hell no! There will be no gay bashing today," I assured him, even though I had already suffered the verbal attack.

The superintendent decided not to move along with the development of the school in 2011. The critics were pleased. Along with the city's LGBT commission and the Newark Pride

Alliance, the organization Bryan voluntarily led as he worked a full-time job, Hetrick-Martin focused its attention on the development of an after-school program for LGBT youth that was housed in a Newark public school. I managed the process. And it was then I understood more clearly why so many of the people I admired pushed back on the school. Some were homophobic, but most had been fighting to keep control of the schools in the hands of the black and Latino residents whose young people relied on them. The state, under the leadership of the white conservative Republican governor, Chris Christie, still controlled Newark Public Schools from Trenton. Governor Christie appointed an outsider, a white woman, as superintendent of a school in a black and Latino city where pride of place and deep connections to Newark were tantamount. They didn't hate me. Their pushback wasn't personal.

They saw me as a representative of a not-for-profit organization many assumed to be endowed with lots of money and led by a white executive from across the Hudson River. Wealthy, white Facebook founder Mark Zuckerberg funded my salary, and the salaries of my colleagues. The $100 million donation Zuckerberg poured into Newark, which was the source of the funding for the proposed new schools, was provided to the surprise of Newark residents. They had no say in determining how the money was to be spent in a district they did not control. They too were weary of existing on the edges of love. They didn't lack care for Newark's youth; they were determined to fight any semblance of manipulation and authoritative rule meted out by the state, the city, and white people in charge of creating the dire social and economic conditions residents were told to be content with.

I placed my bet on my mom when I confessed my truth to the black woman from the black hood who, at the time, lacked a high school diploma. I placed my bet on the strange black man in Newark whose only way of signaling his internal angst was by calling me a "faggot." I placed my bet on the many wise black leaders who saw what I did not, those willing to lose whatever monetary gifts had been dangled before them for the sake of just treatment. And whether I would win or lose, the outcome mattered less than the intention to believe in and radically love black people in a world where we have been denied love.

Black love, shared by so many, is the reason I am here. Breathing. Fighting. Dreaming. Surviving. Working. Even when we start the fires that have consumed so many of our own, I remember who handed us the gasoline, the matches, and the inclination to hate our reflections. OB got his tools from the same place I got mine. We were the same, despite the fact we made different choices. To this day I search for any traces of OB's life on the Internet. I don't know if he's alive and, if he is, I don't know if he's well. But I want him to be free. No more ashes. No more fires. Only love. And the unbridled urgency to build a world where the edges are imagined as the starting place for black liberation now and always.

EPILOGUE

On Saturday, August 9, 2014, an eighteen-year-old black boy's body, which had been pierced by six bullets fired from a white police officer's gun, lay face down and uncovered for nearly four hours on an asphalt-paved street in Ferguson, Missouri. The following night, I couldn't sleep.

Pixelated photos and video captures of the scene were shared widely on social media. I consumed too many and couldn't shake the rage and hurt I felt as I tried to sleep. It was hard to forget the scene at Canfield Drive, where Mike Brown's body rested in blood, in public, in the presence of stunned black neighbors while hordes of mostly white law enforcement officials, including the shooter, Ferguson police officer Darren Wilson, and their dogs kept watch.

So at 4 a.m. on Sunday, I did what most people in this age of smart phones do when they need to escape loneliness or pain. I texted a friend.

I can't sleep, I wrote to Darius Clark Monroe, a brother who lives a short distance from me. We are fairly close, but I'd never contacted him at that hour before. I don't know what compelled me to reach out to him that early morning, but I knew he would understand why I was unable to sleep. I knew he too felt the agonizing pain that has become common when black people's lives are ended by way of extrajudicial killings. Darius responded within seconds. *Bruh, neither can I.*

Neither of us could rid our minds of the death, tears, public lament, and collective anger. We could not unsee the evidence of a contemporary lynching—a lifeless black body on display, and images consumed by a virtual public infatuated by black death.

I wish we could do something. We should gather some folk and drive to St. Louis, I texted.

I'm down. I'll even drive. We can leave tomorrow, Darius replied.

There are roughly 958 miles between Bed-Stuy in Brooklyn, where Darius and I live, and Ferguson, Missouri, where Mike Brown was killed. On any map, the space between the mostly black New York City neighborhood and the St. Louis suburb seems vast. But after Mike Brown's death, Ferguson, a town I hadn't heard of until then, seemed closer than ever. Police abuse, even the kind that is ruled by a court of law as defensible, and its deadly consequences are familiar within black communities. Ferguson was Camden and Bed-Stuy. Ferguson was America. Darius and I wanted to do something, anything, because we had grown tired of containing our rage. We needed to release it.

Sometimes, those of us who are caught in the heavy hands of injustice fight. We refuse to die without a struggle. When the black people in Ferguson began to demand justice for Mike Brown immediately after he was killed, it was clear that they were fighting for us, too. Darius and I needed to stand alongside them.

Darius and I decided against organizing a small impromptu carpool that Monday. We knew it wouldn't be wise to show up in Ferguson without an invitation, proper coordination, or a connection to the people on the ground who had begun to organize. Later that week I called my friend, the organizer and artist Patrisse Cullors. We vented and talked about the idea Darius and I had come up with. She told me she and her LA-based comrades were beginning to organize a ride to Ferguson. We decided to collaborate. Within two weeks, without a budget, working virtually with a team of volunteers across the country, Patrisse and I coordinated what we named the Black Life Matters Freedom Ride to Ferguson that took place on Labor Day weekend 2014. Nearly five hundred people from across the United States and Canada traveled by way of charter buses, vans, or carpools from distances as far as Atlanta, Toronto, and Houston.

There's much to be said about the ride. There are countless people whose labor and donations made it possible. So much has yet to be written about the ways the ride served as a catalyst for new organizing approaches and cross-country connections between organizers and community-based groups. Others will trace the ways the Freedom Ride and other events in Ferguson precipitated the start of the Black Lives Matter Global Network cofounded by Patrisse, Alicia Garza, and Opal Tometi, and championed by founding members from the United States and abroad. What I wish I could adequately detail, though, is the spiritual undercurrent and the radical black love that flowed that weekend. It was a love for black people present among the Ferguson activists who, for more than one hundred days, put their bodies on the line and in the way of rubber bullets and tear gas.

I will always remember standing on the upper level of the host site, the Saint John's United Church of Christ of St. Louis, pastored by the Reverend Starsky Wilson. Looking down from above with my iPhone in hand, I snapped a picture. Nearly five hundred black and brown people filled the sanctuary. They were standing, if they could, with arms extended high above their heads, with fists raised in accord. The group, comprising people who had decided to drive many hours, despite the summer heat, across the country with strangers from their homes to Ferguson, raised fists as a symbol of collective struggle. Their gesture represented a reinvigorated push against the forces of white racial supremacy, aggressive policing, economic oppression, and much else. In the photo, they figured as a collective ready to break open the hands they were contained by. Some people shed tears. Some hugged those closest to them.

I was among a body made up of those who know what it feels like to exist on the edges of the margins. We were black and Latinx and women and men and cisgender and transgender and queer and disabled and formerly incarcerated and hood-raised and southern-bred and fat and without wealth and young and old. We were a version of a beloved community more inclusive than that which MLK himself may have imagined. We made space, though imperfectly, for the contemporary Diane Nashes, Pauli Murrays, and Bayard Rustins during the Freedom Ride. And I will never forget what that moment of collective concern felt like; it felt like freedom.

Throughout my life, sometimes without my awareness, I have been vacillating between the center of the margins and the margins' edges. I've experienced the blunt impact of the various forces, the feet standing on my back, and the hands incarcerating my freedom. In this book, I have tried my best to name what for so long I had only felt: the violent hits by the state, its police force, its educational institutions, its leaders, and the corporate class. Throughout the pages of this book, I have attempted to excavate and narrate my emotional genealogy—the many moments in my life when I took on pain that was never mine, or when I grabbed hold of hope when I needed a reason to survive. I was broken, healed, broken again, and motivated while revisiting the many moments that have helped to shape who I am today: black and free.

Looking back, I realize that my hands have also been used to harm others. My feet were placed on others' necks. I've come to value the practice of critical self-reflection. It is the one practice that has catalyzed internal transformation throughout my life and has made it possible for me to minimize the ways I harmed people I have built relationships and communities with. The Movement for Black Lives' perpetual call for the value of *all* black lives requires critical self-reflection on the part of anyone who claims to be part of the work. It is an act of love and justice to assess the extent to which our ideas and practices suffocate some black people.

I am more hopeful than ever before, not because I believe America will get over its abusive relationship with black people. No. I am hopeful because I have faith in black liberation, which is to say, the freedom we dream and practice when we refuse to set fire to another's potential to love, to laugh, to live. Writing my story was my way of honoring us, of publicly affirming I have survived only because of the grace and care of the people in my life. And even those who have hurt me; I am more determined not to dispose of them today and tomorrow.

Through the Freedom Ride and the subsequent work I've done with the Movement for Black Lives, I've been able to reimagine what a practice of black radical love and justice can look like. In my mind, it looks like my big black family piled up in the tiny house we shared on Broadway in Camden in the 1980s. Always full. Always saturated with love. Always a center of disagreement. Always a place of shelter for those on the edges. Always the place where one could come to make amends and be forgiven. Always a site of imagination where we dreamt of new means of survival in the face of scarcity.

When I think about what it takes to move through and escape the many fires blazing and awaiting black people in America, images of my family, whether congregating in our living room in Camden or in the sanctuary of Saint John's in St. Louis, come to mind. We are the salve, the source, and the water that quenches the fire.

ACKNOWLEDGMENTS

Writing this book has been one of the most challenging and rewarding endeavors I've taken on in my life. The long days of solitude, the times I struggled to capture my thoughts on the page, and the moments of clarity are memories I will forever cherish. And I am grateful for the many people who journeyed alongside me throughout the process.

My family in Camden is the reason this book exists. My story is their story, too. They've trusted me to share it, and they have not once complained. They've only pushed me to get it done. There's no greater love I have yet to experience in life than the love my family has always given me. My only hope is that this book is evidence of me paying the love forward. Diane and Lee Chism, my parents, are my biggest supporters. I pray they, too, continue to live as free and happy as they can. My sisters and brothers, Latasha, Tamisha, Sekeena, Lee, and Rashan, are my hearts. My grandmother and my many aunts, uncles, and cousins remain my first village. I wrote this book to honor them. My cousin Tamara Lewis has kept my life afloat. She has worked as my assistant for several years. I'm certain things have been made easy because of her help. And to my nieces and nephews, seeds of love growing into beautiful human beings, may these words find you when you are ready. Know that you can and will survive, because survival runs through your veins like blood.

Beryl Satter, my friend and mentor, encouraged me to write a memoir several years ago. I feared I had nothing new to offer. I didn't think my life story was worth sharing. But she believed in me. It's because of her faith in my voice that this book is a look inward and not a work of cultural criticism I could hide my heart within.

The publishing world has always appeared distant and vast. I never imagined having access to it until my friends led me to doors that I would not have entered otherwise.

Kiese Laymon, a brother who lives the love he writes about daily, introduced me to his former student and my current agent, Katie Kotchman. His commitment to helping black writers flourish in an industry that hasn't been the most kind to us is unmatched. Katie remains a patient and loving steward of my words. This book, which was once a dream, is here because of her efforts.

Mychal Denzel Smith invited me and a few other writers to read a work in progress at his New York City book launch celebration. He used a day that was supposed to be centered on him as an opportunity to showcase the works of his friends. Who does that but a person who genuinely understands and loves community? I met Nation Books editor Katy O'Donnell at his event. After talking with her over breakfast a few weeks later, I knew Nation Books was the publisher I needed and Katy would be the editor who would help me bring my vision to life. She has done that and so much more. The Nation Books/Hachette team, including Clive Priddle, Alessandra Bastagli, Kristina Fazzalaro, Lindsay Fradkoff, Miguel Cervantes, Stephanie Summerhays, Karen Torres, and Beth Partin, has poured their love into this book. I will never forget the many ways their faith in this project was exampled through their efforts.

Bryan Epps, my best friend, has read every embarrassing and close-to-good iteration of this book. When I feared I wouldn't finish, his assurances encouraged me to stay on course. Allen Frimpong and D'ontace Keyes patiently listened as I read over draft chapters while we vacationed in Cuba. I returned to the United States convinced I had something worth sharing. Dinean Robinson and Joyelle Chandler double as great friends and resourceful supporters. When I needed to laugh more than I cried, they have been on the other end of a text or call, waiting with humor. Fredrick Williams fed my heart and stomach on some of the most difficult days as I wrote. His kindness and joy warmed me when life felt cold. Roslyn and Rhodina Williams, my extended family, have been the big sisters I've always needed. Aimee Meredith Cox was the example I turned to on many occasions for inspiration, and the person I shared wine with on our block when I needed to vent. I watched as she finished her book. She watched as I finished mine.

Joe Osmundson, Jeremiah Grace, Kondor Nunn, Ursula Watson, Tynesha McHarris, Shane Weaver, Marlon Peterson,

Acknowledgments

Wade Davis, Tamura Lomax, Ahmad Greene-Hayes, Guthrie Ramsey, Imani Perry, Hari Ziyad, Zakiya Johnson Lord, Marcie Bianco, Myguail Chappel, Brittney Cooper, Nyle Forte, Patrisse Cullors, dream hampton, Brandon Davis, Janet Mock, James Earl Hardy, Justen Leroy, Lawrence Washington, Paul Daniels II, Ryan Ashley Lowery, Ryan Monroe, Kleaver Cruz, Alicia Garza, Tarell Alvin McCraney, Michael Arceneaux, Kierna Mayo, Jamilah Lemieux, and David Malebranche are just some of the gracious friends who have allowed me to inundate their boxes with drafts or have provided care throughout my writing process. And to the participants in the 2015 Kopkind Retreat and 2017 Read My World International Literary Festival, thank you. Even in solitude, I never felt alone because of their support and presence.

Kemonta Gray has been a quiet force. Even when he didn't know it, he helped me to hold myself together while writing. He helped me to believe in myself. My days in Atlanta, writing in Terrence Cox's beautiful home I was staying in, would have been less memorable and productive had it not been for his presence and constant care.

BLM-NYC is the epitome of radical black love. I will never forget the day they showed up in Camden, without warning, to share space with me and my family as we buried my father. I will always remember the ways they fight every day so black people like my family can live, and do so freely.

To the people I've grown to love in the places that loved me back, from Camden to Newark to Bed-Stuy and Atlanta, thank you. Black folk are gracious as hell. Your grace has kept me alive. To my past and current colleagues at Mic and Urban One, who have supported this project, thank you. The sabbatical and time off to write paid off because of their belief in the necessity of this project. To all who are not mentioned here but are forever in my heart, know that I remember your care.

Special thanks to historian Howard Gillette, author of the groundbreaking *Camden After the Fall: Decline and Renewal in a Post-Industrial City*, whose book centered on Camden taught me so much about the place I call home. Much of the history I've shared in Chapter 1 was uncovered in his stellar work.

NOTES

42 **"And a rush of imagination is our 'flooding'":** Toni Morrison, "The Site of Memory," in *Inventing the Truth: The Art and Craft of Memoir*, 2nd ed., edited by William Zinser (Boston: Houghton Mifflin, 1995), 83–102.

51 **"births out of wedlock" as a social problem:** Barbara Riker, "More and More Pregnant Teen-Agers," *Los Angeles Times*, April 18, 1976. Accessed online.

51 **birthrate for unmarried white women has since steadily increased:** Child Trends Databank Indicator, "Birthrates to Unmarried Women," accessed August 14, 2017, https://www.childtrends.org/indicators/births-to-unmarried-women/.

71 **Princeton spent over $8,000:** "School Funding," *PBS NewsHour*, accessed August 20, 2017, https://www.pbs.org/newshour/education/education-july-dec96-school_funding_10-03.

73 **the district suffered from a lack of instructional resources:** Kevin Riordan, "Report Condemns Lack of Resources," *Courier-Post*, December 23, 1990.

77 **I wasn't prepared for a beating:** Portions of this section originally appeared in my article "Black, LGBT, American: A Search for Sanctuaries," *The Advocate*, July 15, 2013, available online at https://www.advocate.com/print-issue/current-issue/2013/07/15/black-gay-american.

84 **nobodies caught up in web of interconnected oppression:** Marc Lamont Hill, *Nobody: Casualties of America's War on the Vulnerable, from Ferguson to Flint and Beyond* (New York: Atria Books, 2016), xix.

88 **The median income:** United States Census Bureau, *Money Income of Households, Families, and Persons in the United States: 1990*, August

1991, accessed August 28, 2017, https://www2.census.gov/prod2/popscan/p60-174.pdf.

101 **"What Homosexuals Do":** 101 Cong. Rec. H3511 (daily ed. June 29, 1989) (remarks of Rep. William Dannemeyer).

119 **At the end of 1994, 1,053,738 people were incarcerated:** Allen J. Beck and Darrell K. Gilliard, *Prisoners in 1994*, statistical report prepared for the annual bulletin of the Bureau of Justice Statistics, US Department of Justice, August 17, 1995, https://www.bjs.gov/index.cfm?ty=pbdetail&iid=1280.

120 **the 1,104,074 people caged within its institutions:** US Department of Justice, Bureau of Justice Statistics, "State and Federal Prisons Report Record Growth During Last 12 Months," press release no. 202/307-0784, December 3, 1995, https://www.bjs.gov/content/pub/pdf/pam95.pdf.

DARNELL L. MOORE is an editor-at-large at CASSIUS, a digital platform of Urban One, a columnist at LogoTV.com and *NewNowNext*, a co–managing editor at *The Feminist Wire*, and a contributor at *Mic*, where he hosted their widely viewed digital series The Movement. He writes regularly for *Ebony*, the *Advocate*, *Vice*, and the *Guardian*. Moore was one of the original Black Lives Matter organizers who co-organized bus trips from New York to Ferguson after the murder of Michael Brown. Moore is a writer-in-residence at the Center on African-American Religion, Sexual Politics, and Social Justice at Columbia University; has taught at NYU, Rutgers, Fordham, and Vassar; and was trained at Eastern University and Princeton Theological Seminary. In 2016, he was named one of The Root 100, and in 2015 he was named one of *Ebony*'s Power 100 and Planned Parenthood's 99 Dream Keepers. He divides his time between Brooklyn and Atlanta.